CHINA

The
Business Traveller's
Handbook

China
The Business Traveller's Handbook

First published in 2003 by
Interlink Books
An imprint of Interlink Publishing Group, Inc.
46 Crosby Street, Northampton, Massachusetts 01060
www.interlinkbooks.com

ISBN 1-56656-495-6

Library of Congress Cataloging-in-Publication Data available

The author and publisher have made every effort to ensure that the facts in this handbook are accurate and up-to-date. The reader is advised, however, to verify travel and visa arrangements with the appropriate consular office prior to departure. The author and publisher cannot accept any responsibility for loss, injury or inconvenience, however caused.

None of the maps in this book are designed to have any political significance.

Printed and bound in Singapore by Tien Wah Press

To request our complete 40-page full-color catalog, please call us toll free at 1-800-238-LINK, visit our website at www.interlinkbooks.com or send us an e-mail: info@interlinkbooks.com

PICTURE CREDITS: *All photographs by* Ian Smith

China

The Business Travellers' Handbook

Bernard Dennis MBE

Top: the souvenir stands earn a steady trade on the parapets of the Great Wall of China, the country's leading tourist attraction.

Bottom: Tiananmen Square in Beijing, showing the Great Hall of the People and Chairman Mao's mausoleum, is testament to the grandeur of the Communist vision.

Top: gambling in the streets and parks is a regular passtime in China.

Bottom left: rikshaws are still the most popular form of transport in the cities, now powered by pedals rather than towed by man on foot.

Bottom right: the Temple of Heaven, the Hall of Prayer for Good Harvests.

Above: inside the Forbidden City – the Hall of Supreme Harmony, shows traditional Chinese architecture in all its majesty with (above right) consistent attention to detail as shown by this section of the beautiful marble staircase.

Bottom left: the national flag of the PRC is a clear Communist red, emblem of the Cultural Revolution commemorated widely (bottom right) in statues and posters.

Acknowledgements

I am indebted to the many people who have, perhaps unknowingly, provided me with the information about China and Hong Kong over the past 12 years or so.

I should also like to thank my wife Stephanie and daughter Imogen for their help and support whilst I have travelled extensively on business.

Thanks also go to Ian Smith, journalist and tourist, who provided the photographs.

CONTENTS

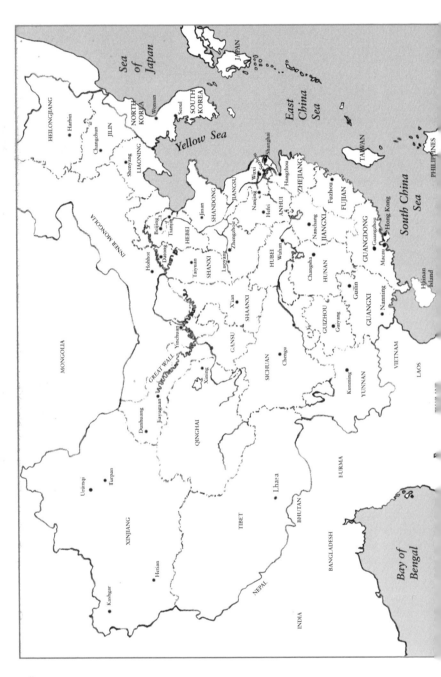

China

1

China yesterday and today

China yesterday and today

Overview of a Nation

For more than 2,000 years China has developed a civilisation which has endured longer than any other in history, and today is the most populous country in the world. It is a vast, complex and multicultural nation.

The capital is Beijing (still referred to as Peking by the British Embassy) and other major cities include Shanghai, Tianjin, Shenyang, Wuhan, Guangzhou (Canton), Chongqing, Harbin and Chengdu. China is made up of 22 provinces and four special municipalities and also encompasses five Autonomous Regions, including Tibet, and two Special Administrative Regions, Hong Kong, handed over from British rule in 1997, and Macau, formerly a Portuguese colony and handed over in 1999.

Geography

Geographically, climatically and culturally diverse, it is a land of great beauty and rich heritage. Its landmass of 9,596 sq km holds a population of 1.3 billion (approximately 25 per cent of the world population) of which the vast majority are Han, or ethnic Chinese. There are 55 recognised minority groups, mostly scattered through the sparsely settled border areas.

China's 49 degrees of latitude encompasses a climate ranging from subarctic to tropical, with altitudes ranging from the peak of Mount Everest, the world's highest mountain (8,847m), to the Turpan Depression at 154m below sea level.

Population

At the end of 2001, the population of the four major urban conglomerations, including the surrounding counties, stood at Beijing 13.8 million, Chongqing 31m, Shanghai 16.1m and Tianjin 10m.

Language

The Chinese language has two written forms and the classical style is reserved for official documents. The official spoken language is Mandarin (Putonghua) although there are many other dialects throughout the country. In southern China and Hong Kong the dominant dialect is Cantonese and as such a person from the south, speaking Cantonese, may not be able to understand a northerner whose main language will be

1

Mandarin, yet they will be able to write to each other and fully understand the written characters. This is because the Chinese written characters do not represent sounds or phonetics as our words do. They are more like pictures, with each picture meaning the same to any Chinese, be he from the far north or in Hong Kong. These characters are referred to as ideographs, as they represent ideas, not names. There are over 40,000 characters but in ordinary everyday reading it is only necessary to know about 3,000. It is fascinating to watch office workers and secretaries using their computers, typing sometimes four characters which, with the benefit of modern computer software, converts those four characters into one understandable character, just like a form of shorthand. After 1949 simplified symbols were introduced in order to simplify the written language, although the traditional script is still used in Hong Kong and Taiwan. Pinyin, the Latin transcription of Standard Chinese, is used in dictionaries and in street names, etc.

Religion

Under the present system all religions have to be registered with the State and the official policy is to tolerate but not encourage religion.

Today, the indigenous religions are Confucianism, Taoism and Buddhism. In addition there are Muslim and Christian minorities. The ethical teachings of Confucius (Kong Fuzi) in the 6th century BC stressed duty and submission to authority. Taoism was derived from the teachings of the sage Lao-tsu (Laozi) and others. Buddhism was introduced from India at the time of Christ and spread in the following centuries, developing its own branch of Mahayana Buddhism with Tibetan Buddhism, or Lamaism, prevailing in Tibet and Inner Mongolia.

Now China has some 13,000 Buddhist temples and 200,000 monks and nuns. During the Tang and Song dynasties Arab and Persian merchants brought Islam overland along the Silk Road into Northwest China and by sea to the coastal cities in the Southeast. Islam flourished at the time of the Mongol empire, and now China has some 30,000 mosques and more than 40,000 imams and ahungs. Christianity was introduced to China on a large scale after the Opium Wars. Now there are about 4 million Catholic believers, 4,000 clergy and 4,600 churches, 10 million Protestants, 18,000 clergy and over 12,000 churches and 25,000 other centres of worship.

During the Cultural Revolution all forms of religious worship were banned. Religious observance is now tolerated in spite of government distrust of any allegiance to an outside power such as the Pope or the Dalai Lama, or the leader of the banned Falun Gong cult, but this is a topic best not discussed when visiting China.

Agriculture

The first impression of this vast land is that it is primarily an agricultural country. Aside from the mountain ranges of the west and the deserts of the north which comprise two-thirds of the country, much of the land along the great rivers is immensely fertile and is worked with extreme care. The use of hand ploughs and oxen still survive.

The one food that typifies China is rice. This is grown in southern and central China with millet, wheat and barley in abundance in northern China. Tea is grown in the highlands of central China, on the coast and also in Szechwan. China is also famous for its silk, which is produced from Shantung to Guangzhou (Canton). Other crops such as sugar, cotton, tobacco and soya bean are important to the economy but one of the most commonly grown and used products is bamboo. You have to marvel at the incredible structures of bamboo scaffolding that surround modern buildings under construction. Bamboo is probably the most versatile of materials and is used extensively.

Customs

For centuries upper class Chinese bound the feet of their daughters so tightly from the age of five that their feet ceased to grow and the toes curled under and the bones were deformed. As a result, and at the cost of great suffering, many upper-class women walked on stumps of feet and were practically helpless.

After the overthrow of the Manchu dynasty in 1911, men began to cut off their "queues" or pigtails which were originally worn under compulsion as a sign of submission to those rulers. (Compare recent events in Afghanistan and the power of the Taliban.) China has passed laws forbidding both these practices, although some cases still exist as old habits and traditions die hard.

1

A Brief History of China

The history of China is the history of successions of dynasties rising and falling, bringing progress and then inevitably disintegrating. The peasantry, poverty-stricken, overtaxed and deprived of rights, finally rise up in rebellion against a weakened corrupt dynasty. Strife and wars, together with foreign incursions, natural disasters, follow and the kingdoms break up until another strong ruler emerges. At the same time, extraordinary art, literature and science is produced, both in times of war and peace.

During the last 2,000 years China, with its sophisticated administration and culture was far ahead in civilisation from the barbaric West. And yet in later centuries it was these 'foreign devils' as they were known to the Chinese who became superior in trade and war. The 19th century industrial revolutions in the Western countries spurred them on to exploit and profit from China's wealth. Meanwhile the Middle Kingdom, the Chinese name for their country, was declining, becoming more and more closed and inward looking, and powerless to prevent these foreign incursions. But towards the end of the 19th century the exploitation by foreign powers, combined with a decaying, autocractic and remote imperial dynasty, was producing a new sense of nationalism and egalitarianism.

The 20th century brought revolution and an end to thousands of years of imperial rule. Attempts were made to find a Marxist solution to the problem of governing and controlling such a vast population and the land they occupied. The country endured Japanese invasion, civil war, devastating famines amd natural disasters. Disastrous experiments in economic centralisation which brought misery to millions have now been overturned but have brought fresh problems from urbanisation and industrialisation. Economic zones have been allowed and brought an improved standard of living to millions, yet China remains a country of over 700 million peasants working in the rural areas, with the vast majority of urban workers employed by heavily-subsidised and often grossly inefficient State Owned Enterprises (SOEs). The vast population remains subservient to a centralised government and poverty is widespread. However, China has not repeated the mistakes of Russia, which has suffered from a too rapid pace of reform. Reform, political and economic, is proceeding gradually, and China, the last great world empire, is growing more powerful and self confident. Now seriously competing with its Asian neighbours through its astonishingly rapid economic expansion, matching the West in technology, in military and nuclear might, China is likely soon to become the real superpower of the world.

Ancient History

The earliest recorded Chinese dynasty, the Xia Dynasty, is believed to date from 2000-1500 BC, followed by the bronze age feudal Shang Dynasty (1500-1066 BC), which was eventually overthrown by the iron age Zhou Dynasty (1066-221 BC). The worship of Heaven and the emperor as the Son of Heaven and the worship of ancestors was practised. During the latter part of this dynasty, known as the Warring States period, the country broke up into small kingdoms (403-221 BC). This was the time of Confucius (Kong Zi, 551-479 BC) and Lao-Tse, the founder of Taoism.

Qin Dynasty (221-206 BC)

In 221 BC the despotic emperor Qin Shi Huangdi united the individual states into one empire, founding the Qin Dynasty (or Ch'in Dynasty, from which the name of China is derived). His tomb, together with over 7,000 terracotta soldiers, a vivid illustration of the armies of the time, was discovered in 1974. Under the Qin Dynasty, the old feudal system was abolished and replaced by administrative districts under the influence of the Legalists. Confucianism was persecuted and books destroyed. Roads, canals, and the Silk Road were established and weights and measures, currency, and writing was standardised, but the emperor's harsh rule made him hated by the Chinese.

The Great Wall of China

Begun in the 3rd century BC by the Emperor Qin Shi Huangdi to keep out northern nomadic tribes, and greatly extended during the Ming Dynasty against the Mongols, the Great Wall of China is the most famous single structure in China, if not in the world. It is 2,200 km (1,400 miles) long, constructed mainly of brick and masonry and built across northern China over mountains and through very difficult terrain. Half a million workers are estimated to have worked on its

1

construction. Stretching from Shanhaiguan on the shores of the Yellow Sea to the borders of Kansu and Chinese Turkistan in the West, the Great Wall crosses high mountains and deep valleys. It is an amazing feat of engineering considering the lack of modern technology available at the time of construction and is said to be visible from the moon. It is still in pretty good shape, assuming of course that you ignore the tourist "attractions" that have mushroomed around it in recent years at its nearest point to Beijing!

Han Dynasty (206 BC to AD 220)
Under the Han Dynasty in the 3rd century AD, Confucian philosophy was revived, Buddhism was introduced, and the system of examinations to recruit civil servants was begun which lasted till the 19th century. Paper was invented and art and literature flourished and trade increased along the Silk Road. Chinese silks reached the Roman Empire. Peasant rebellions and Taoist "Yellow Turbans" brought the dynasty to an end.

The Three Kingdoms (220-581)
The country was divided into the Wei, Chu and Wu, but the Northern and Southern Wei Dynasties forming the Jin Dynasty (265-439) predominated.

Inspite of the incessant wars of this period, art and poetry flourished. The famous Buddhist caves of Dunhuang, Luoyang and Yungang date from this period.

Tang Dynasty (618-907)
After centuries of anarchy, warring tribes and foreign incursions, the repressive Sui Dynasty (581-618) unified China once again and was followed by the Tang Dynasty, when China enjoyed a Golden Age, with Xi'an as the capital. Law and order was restored, arts — particularly ceramics and poetry — and sciences flourished. Buddhist sacred texts were introduced. Trade and industry developed. The empire expanded to include Central Asia and Tibet, but the dynasty declined and was eventuallly overcome by peasant revolts.

Northern and Southern Song Dynasties (960-1279)
After the country had once more been engulfed in war, these rulers gave China peace, prosperity and cultural enrichment. Literature and painting flourished in this period, whose notable achievements were the invention of saltpetre, gunpowder, fireworks, printing and porcelain.

The Mongol Empire (the Yuan Dynasty, 1279-1368)

In 1279 Ghengis Khan and the Mongols conquered China, creating an enormous empire under the Emperor Kublai Khan, Genghis Khan's grandson, who made Beijing (Khanbaliq) his winter residence. Mongol fleets sailed to the Indian Ocean and the South Seas. The first that Europe really knew of Cathay (as China was called in the Middle Ages) was from the Venetian traveller, Marco Polo (1254-1324), who journeyed overland to China and served for 17 years under Kublai Khan. The repressed Chinese eventually succeeded in overthrowing the dynasty.

Ming Dynasty (1368-1644)

The Ming Dynasty restored Chinese rule, with its two strong emperors Hongwu and Yongle, who moved the capital from Nanjing to Beiping (Northern Peace) renaming it Beijing (Northern Capital). The eastern section of the Great Wall was restored to prevent further Mongol invasion. Although Chinese ships sailed as far as Madagascar, the Mandarin period saw an increasing isolationism prevail, reacting against repeated incursions from Mongols, Japanese and Europeans. It was to be the last indigenous Chinese dynasty. The Ming Dynasty is famous for its imperial architecture, and for its style of fine porcelain.

Qing Dynasty (1644-1911)

With the decline of the Ming Dynasty, once again China fell under foreign rule. A peasant revolt led to invasion by the Manchus from the north. Under the Manchus, who united Manchuria with China, and annexed more territories, the country became crystallised and isolated from outside influence. Their dynasty, the Qing, was to be China's last imperial dynasty.

This was the time of the Industrial Revolution in Europe and the temptation and opportunities for business and trade with an emerging country of hitherto untapped wealth were enormous to the Western countries.

The Treaty of Nanking (1842)

Many commercial advantages were gained by the Western powers as a result of the Treaty of Nanking which brought to an end the first Opium War and gave Hong Kong to the British. China failed to stop the lucrative opium trade and was compelled to open five "treaty ports" to Western trade and pay a war

1

indemnity. These increased to a total of 69 ports where foreigners were allowed to reside, own property and conduct business. One of the main "treaty ports" was Shanghai and the British and French set up the first foreign concessions in the city, the British along the Bund on the banks of the Huangpu River and also an area to the north of the old Chinese city. The Americans set up concessions in 1863, the Japanese in 1895 and these merged with the British concession to form an International Settlement. These privileges, resented by the Chinese as the "Unfair Treaties", were relinquished in 1943.

More Recent History

The Manchu dynasty succeeded in suppressing the internal Taiping Rebellion (1850-64), but from 1860 to 1894 China was subjected to increasing foreign pressure and in 1895 was defeated in war with Japan (1894-95). Formosa was lost to the Japanese. It was an object lesson to China as to what the adoption of Western ways might do towards increasing the military power of an Oriental nation. The intelligent and free thinking element of the Chinese population began to realise that the only way forward to resist foreign aggression was by internal reform. Having lost Korea to Japan, Kiaochow to Germany and Port Arthur to Russia, it was becoming clear that modernisation was essential to China's survival. The young emperor Ku'ang Hsu and his advisers were issuing edicts from Peking intending to modernise China but the ultimate result was to galvanise the Dowager Empress Tze-Hsi to furious action and retribution. She seized power, imprisoned the emperor, had many of the reformers executed and abolished all reforms.

The Boxer Rebellion (1900)

Fanatical bands of "Boxers" pledged to depose and persecute foreigners and Christians, whom they saw as barbarians annexing their land, and the Dowager Empress isssued an amazing order that all foreigners should be killed! This provoked the entry of foreign troops into Peking and the interim court fled. The European powers dictated severe restrictive terms. Fortifications were razed to the ground, the Summer Palace was destroyed, formal apologies were demanded, which to the Chinese was an embarrassing "loss of face", and a heavy indemnity was imposed. The news of Japan's victory over Russia in 1905 created a greater demand for change in China.

The last Emperor
In 1908 both the Emperor Ku'ang Hsu and the Dowager Empress Tze-Hsi died, ironically within a day of each other, and the Emperor's two-year-old nephew, Pu Yi, came to the throne as Hsuan T'ung, with the baby's father Prince Chun controlling the regency. Meanwhile hardship and poverty were increasing in China.

Revolution and Republic
A revolution was inevitable and in 1911 Dr Sun Yat-sen led the revolt which overthrew the Manchu dynasty and created the Republic of China. One of the most important figures in China's modern history, Dr Sun Yat-sen is venerated as the Father of the Revolution and was China's first President. Dr Sun Yat-sen's party, the Kuomintang (KMT, later known as the Nationalist Party) hoped to modernise the country while at the same time freeing it from Western political domination.

Fearing civil war, however, Dr Sun Yat-sen resigned in favour of Yuan Shi-Kai, a Manchu general and warlord, who had been Viceroy under the Dowager Empress, but in 1913 the KMT rose against him. Yuan Shi-Kai crushed the revolt but died in 1916 before realising his dream of restoring the monarchy with himself as emperor. In 1917 the KMT denounced the Peking government as illegal and set up a provisional government in Canton (Guangzhou) headed by Dr Sun Yat-sen.

Rise of CCP and Mao Zedong
In 1921 Mao Zedong and other Marxists founded the Chinese Communist Party (CCP) which evolved out of the student May Fourth Movement. Dr Sun Yat-sen once more became President but died in 1925, his place being taken by General Chiang Kai-shek, his able protegé and lieutenant, who instigated a purge of Communists. Much happened under the rule of Chiang KaiShek; the seat of government changed, Nanking became the capital in 1928 but was replaced by Chungking in 1937 when the Japanese invaded China and occupied Peking.

Years of famine in the country increased discontent and led more Chinese to support the Communists. The Nationalists laid siege to the Red Army at Ruijin. To

1

escape the KMT, Mao Zedong led his CCP forces, some 100,000 men and women, on the famous 6,000 mile (10,000 km) journey known as the Long March to Shanxi Province in 1934. A year later, surviving starvation, harsh conditions and attacks from the KMT, only one-tenth of Mao's army reached Yan'an in Shaaxi province.

World War II
The Japanese invasion of China and occupation of Peking in 1937 forced the CCP and KMT to combine against the common enemy. Japan surrendered to the Allies in 1945 after occupying large areas of China.

Chinese Civil War (1945-49)
After the war, a bitter civil war raged in China between the CCP and the KMT. By the end of 1949 Chungking, Nanking and canton had fallen to the Communists. General Li Tsung-jen became President after Chiang Kai-shek's resignation. In December 1949 General Li went to the USA for medical treatment and it was decided to move the Nationalist Government to Taipei, capital of Formosa, now known as Taiwan.

People's Republic of China (1949)
The victorious Chinese Communist Party led by Mao Zedong declared the People's Republic of China (PRC) in October 1949 and eventually gained control of the whole of China, expelling foreigners and foreign enterprises. The post war-years were dominated by the question of official recognition of the government of Communist China at the expense of the old regime in Taiwan.

Mao took over a country poverty stricken and underdeveloped. The Agrarian Law of 1950 began the redistribution of land to the peasants and a series of government campaigns to create a new China were introduced to eradicate old ideas, habits, customs and culture (the Four Olds), to eliminate corruption and crime, to denounce religion, and to make art and literature serve the people.

The Great Leap Forward (1958-61)
Mao's brief period of openness in 1956 of 'Let a Hundred Flowers Bloom' was quickly replaced by a crackdown on independent political thought.

Mao aimed to overcome the backwardness of China's economy, industry and technology with 'The Great Leap

Forward'. However, it is estimated that over 30 million people starved to death as a result of his economic collectivisation programme begun in 1958 and the natural disasters in 1960-61.

The Cultural Revolution (1966-76)
In 1966 Mao instigated the Great Proletarian Cultural Revolution, which lasted 10 years and subjected the people to terror, persecution, poverty and the terrifying "persuasive" methods of the Red Guards. It was during this time, in 1967, that the British Embassy was invaded by a raging mob which set the building on fire (see the memoirs of the British Charge D'affaires (later Ambassador) Percy Craddock, "Experiences of China").

Chairman Mao was elevated to a status of almost demigod proportions and even today you will see evidence of his influence wherever you travel within China.

Deng Xiaoping and reform programme
Chairman Mao died in 1976. He had been a unifying force in China but after his death a power struggle ensued. The Gang of Four which included Mao's wife failed in their bid to seize power. Zhou Enlai and Deng Xiaoping launched China's economic reform programme. China became less isolated, some private enterprise and religious freedom was restored. Special Economic Zones outside the socialist economy were created to attract foreign investment. But political freedom was slow to follow economic liberalism, and the conservative party leadership were not moving quickly enough for the students.

Tiananmen Square (1989)
In 1989 the pro-democracy student movement culminated in a showdown in Tiananmen Square, Beijing, when hundreds of students were killed by Chinese troops.

Jiang Zemin
In 1993, Jiang Zemin was appointed President of PRC. Jiang and the new premier, Zhu Rongji, were both former Mayors of Shanghai. Interestingly, after 1949 Shanghai remained a centre of radicalism. Mao, stifled by the bureaucracy in Beijing, launched the Cultural Revolution in Shanghai in 1966. After the death of Mao in 1976, Shanghai was the last stronghold of the Gang of

1

Four in their struggle for succession, although their planned coup never materialised.

Since 1949 and the founding of the PRC, many changes occurred, from times of political openness and burgeoning economic development to retrenchment and a desire to maintain its own identity in terms of rejecting "western influence". The CCP was the dominant political party and despite proper means of communication with the outside world, China managed to establish an economic system which ultimately succeeded in raising the standard of living, people's incomes and averting China's terrible and prevalent famines.

In November 2002, the President, Jiang Zemin, was replaced as General Secretary of the Chinese Communist Party by Vice-President Hu Jintao, who is also expected to take over the post of President at the National People's Congress in March 2003. Wen Jiabao is expected to replace Zhu Rongji as premier at the same time. Mr Jiang will retain the powerful post of head of the Party's Central Military Commission, just as Mr Deng did before him, and although 76, beyond the retirement age of 70, is expected to remain an influential and powerful elder statesman.

Hong Kong SAR

Hong Kong, "the merchant city", has been called "the conveyor belt for goods between China and the rest of the world". Other quotations from the latter part of the 20th century include: "a borrowed place living on borrowed time", and "cargo is the essence of Hong Kong".

Until the handover in 1997, Hong Kong, was a British Crown Colony, governed by the British Government with a Governor as the representative of the Crown.

The first governor of Hong Kong was Admiral Sir Charles Elliot, who declared himself governor of Britain's first colonial acquisition in the Far East in 1841 whilst on board HMS Wellesley, which was moored just off Hong Kong island. The same day, 26 January, Captain Edward Belcher RN with the occupying force raised the Union Jack flag on Hong Kong and hence started the history of Hong Kong as we know it today.

But at the time the British first raised the Union Jack flag on Hong Kong in 1841 it was considered by British Foreign Secretary Lord Palmerston merely a "barren island". One wonders what his reaction would be now to the subsequent development of this relatively small but significant patch of land!

The 30 square miles (78 sq km) of Hong Kong Island became a British Crown Colony after the Treaty of Nanking (1842) which ended the first Opium War. After the second Opium War, Britain acquired the southern tip of Kowloon in 1860 at the Convention of Peking, about 15 square miles of the Chinese mainland, as a base for a military garrison. Hong Kong by now was established as a British Trading Station and a minor entrepôt in the Far East. After the Japanese invaded China in 1895 Britain was able to extract a further concession from the Chinese and in 1898 secured a 99-year lease on what was known as the New Territories which consisted of 287 square miles and 235 small and mainly uninhabited islands around Hong Kong. This agreement was to expire on 1 July 1997.

At the beginning of the People's Republic, the Communists were flushed with success but stopped short of crossing the border, or 'bamboo curtain' and overrunning Hong Kong. The PRC made it very clear they rejected the "unequal treaties' by which Hong Kong had been partitioned from China in 1841 and added that the situation could be resolved by discussion and negotiation at a later date.

In subsequent years, it became more apparent that successive Chinese governments were "embarrassed" and "humiliated" by the loss of Hong Kong and the memories of 1840 and "unequal treaties" were always uppermost in the minds of the Chinese leaders. It became obvious that China's determination to recover their national territory and eliminate past humiliations was a main priority. This had a strong impact on British diplomacy right up to the arrival of Chris Pattern, the last governor of Hong Kong, in July 1992.

In 1980 the Chinese leader Deng Xiaoping coined the phrase "one country, two systems" to emphasise the relationship between the 1.3 billion population on the Chinese mainland and the 6 million inhabitants of Hong

Kong. This phrase, or slogan, appealed to the masses and became their doctrine for the way ahead when eventually Hong Kong reverted to China.

In 1984 the UK and China signed a Joint Declaration agreeing to the handover of Hong Kong on 1 July 1997. The Joint Declaration guaranteed the free movement of goods and capital; the retention of Hong Kong's free port status; a separate customs territory and freely convertible currency; the protection of property rights and foreign investment; the right of free movement to and from Hong Kong; autonomy in the conduct of its external commercial relations and its own monetary and financial policies; and judicial independence. Hong Kong's constitution is the Basic Law passed by China in 1990 guaranteeing the system will remain unchanged for 50 years.

The last British Governor of Hong Kong, Chris Patten, endeavoured to extend democracy in the Colony before the handover, much to the irritation of the Chinese Government. The political and diplomatic issues leading up to the handover of Hong Kong in 1997 are well covered in Jonathan Dimbleby's book, *The Last Governor*.

The handover of Hong Kong in 1997 was greeted with national celebrations across China. An official three-day public holiday was declared as Hong Kong became a Special Administrative Region (SAR) within China. Since then Hong Kong has surprised the world by continuing to enjoy a vibrant economy within the Republic.

The Chief Executive of Hong Kong SAR is Tung Chee-Hwa, a former businessman, aided by an Executive Council and Legislative Council. The Chief Secretary for Administration is Donald Tsang.

Macau

Macau is situated on a small peninsula at the mouth of the Pearl River delta and is linked to the Chinese mainland by an isthmus known as the Ferreira do Amaral. There are two smaller islands, Taipa and Coloane, connected to the main territory by a bridge and causeway. Founded by the Portuguese in 1557, Macau declined as a regional trading centre in the early 19th century with the rise of Hong Kong which had the advantage of a deep water port. In 1887 China recognised Portuguese sovereignty over Macau. There was no time constraint in handing back the territory to the Chinese. Negotiations began in the 1980s for the handover which was agreed in 1987 and effected in 1999 when Macau became the Macau Special Administrative Region of China governed by a Chief Executive, assisted by Executive and Legislative Councils.

Taiwan

Taiwan (formerly Formosa) was inhabited by the Chinese until the 17th century, it was occupied by Dutch and Spanish and then by supporters of the deposed Ming Dynasty in the 17th century, and by the Qing Dynasty in 1885, when it was declared an official province of China. It came under the control of Japan after the first Sino-Japanese war until it was returned in 1945. When Mao Zedong founded the People's Republic of China in 1949, Chiang Kai-Shek and the KMT fled to Taiwan, retaining the name of Republic of China. No longer recognised by the UN since 1971, the island has suffered both from the 1997 "Asian Crash" and more recently with a devastating earthquake. Nevertheless its economy is well developed and it remains an important manufacturing base and supplier in the Far East region.

The relationship between the People's Republic of China and Taiwan (Republic of China) remains very sensitive although surprisingly there is a considerable amount of trade between the two countries. Life always goes on and always will when trade is involved! Now a thriving democracy, Taiwan elected the first non-KMT President, Chen Shui-bian of the Democratic Progressive Party (DPP) in 2000.

In 1999 tension between the PRC and Taiwan increased considerably when the former Taiwanese President, Lee Teng-hui described Taiwan's relationship with China as "state to state". This statement was later adopted as the official policy by the ruling KMT. The Chinese on the other hand are looking to establish a "One China" principle with Taiwan rather than recognising the "state to state" idea and the rhetoric continues which will hopefully result in an agreement from which neither side will lose "face".

1

Tibet (Xijang)

A remote, hidden country on the 'Roof of the World' surrounded by the world's highest mountains, remained impenetrable to Western travellers until the 19th century. Tibetan Lamaism, a form of Buddhism, which had been introduced in the 7th century, led to the country being ruled by Lama priest-kings with the Dalai Lama as the spiritual and temporal head. Tibet became a vassal state under China during the Mongol dynasty.

Although for most of the 20th century Tibet enjoyed a virtual independence, the Chinese had never given up their historical claims to the country, and in 1950 invaded and set up a military and administrative headquarters. After the failure of several uprisings against Chinese rule, the Dalai Lama and thousands of his followers fled to India in 1959. Agriculture was collectivised and Lamaism suppressed. During the Cultural Revolution many monasteries and historic monuments were destroyed. Tibet was declared an Autonomous Region of China in 1965, and Chinese immigration was encouraged. Recently efforts have been made by the Chinese to improve the lot of the Tibetans, religious freedom has been reinstated, monasteries restored and trade and industry promoted, but greater autonomy is still desired by the population and the country remains one of the poorest in the world.

Notable Historical Events in China

6000-4000 BC	Archaeological evidence of fishing and farming activities in Southern China
2000-1500 BC	Xia Dynasty
1500-1066 BC	Shang Dynasty
1066-221 BC	Zhou Dynasty
221-206	First Emperor of China, Qin Shi Huangdi, unites country and gives China its name. (Ts'in Dynasty) The Great Wall of China begun.
206-AD220	Han Dynasty
220-581	The Three Kingdoms
581-618	Sui Dynasty
618-907	Tang Dynasty

960-1279	Song Dynasties
1279-1368	Mongols invade China and form the Yuan Dynasty. Jenghis Khan conquers northern China and grandson Kublai Khan becomes Mongol emperor of whole of China
13th cent	Marco Polo visits China or Cathay as it was known in the West
1368-1644	Ming Dynasty
1406-20	Building of the Imperial Palace at Beijing during the reign of the Emperor Yongle
1516	The Portuguese arrive in Canton

15th to 17th centuries - rebuilding of the Great Wall

1644-1911	Qing Dynasty - China ruled by the Manchus of Manchuria
1839-42	First Opium War
1842	The Treaty of Nanking (Nanjing). Chinese ports forced to open to foreign trade and Hong Kong ceded to Britain
1850-64	Taiping Rebellion against the Qing Dynasty suppressed
1856-58	Second Opium War ends with Treaty of Tientsin (Tianjin): Britain establishes permanent diplomatic representation in Peking.
1860	Further hostilities result in the destruction of the Imperial Summer Palace by Anglo-French forces
1894-95	War with Japan, resulting in defeat for China
1900	The Boxer Rebellion sparked by concessions gained by foreign powers. Siege of foreign legations in Beijing who are rescued by international forces

1

1908	Dowager Empress Cixi (Tze-Hsi) dies. Child Pu Yi proclaimed Emperor Hsuan T'ung
1912	Revolution removes boy Emperor. Republic of China proclaimed.
	Dr Sun Yat-sen becomes first President of China
1921	Chinese Communist Party (CCP) founded
1925	Death of Dr Sun Yat-sen
1923-31	First United Front between CCP and KMT (Kuomintang - Nationalist Party)
1934-35	CCP forces retreat from KMT in the Long March. 10,000 out of 100,000 survive the 6,000-mile journey.
1937	Japan invades China. Second United Front between KMT and CCP
1945	World War II ends with the defeat of Japan by the Allies
1945-49	Chinese Civil War
1949	People's Liberation Army takes Shanghai. People's Republic of China (PRC) founded by Mao Zedong who is elected Chairman. Nationalists withdraw to Taiwan (Formosa)
1950	China invades Tibet
1959	Dalai Lama flees to India
1960	Soviet Union and China in conflict. USSR economic aid ceases
1958-61	The "Great Leap Forward" results in famine killing 30 million Chinese
1966-76	Cultural Revolution
1971	The United Nations Assembly replaces the Republic of China (Taiwan) with the People's Republic of China.

1

1972	US President Richard Nixon visits China
1976	Death of Mao and Premier Zhou Enlai
1978	Deng Xiaoping launches China's reform programme
1979	USA formally recognises People's Republic of China
1989	Suppression of the pro-democracy movement in Tiananmen Square, Beijing. Jiang Zemin appointed as General Secretary of the CCP.
1993	Jiang Zemin appointed President of PRC
1994	China tests two atomic bombs
1996	The largest trade mission (270 businessmen and women) ever to leave UK shores departs for Beijing, Shanghai and Hong Kong led by Michael Heseltine, Deputy Prime Minister
1997	Death of Deng Xiaoping. Hong Kong returns to China
2000	Reform programme continues
2002	New leadership: President Jiang Zemin replaced by Hu Jintao

Notable Historical Events in Hong Kong

1841	British arrive in Hong Kong and Admiral Sir Charles Elliot declares himself governor from on board
HMS	Wellesley
1842	Treaty of Nanking ends first Opium War and secures British sovereignty over Hong Kong
1843	Hong Kong formally declared a British Crown Colony
1860	The Convention of Peking cedes southern tip of Kowloon to Britain

1864	Hong Kong and Shanghai Bank (HSBC) is founded
1888	Funicular tramway to the Peak on Hong Kong Island is built
1898	Britain extracts a further concession with a 99-year lease on the New Territories to end on 1 July 1997
1911	Chinese refugees pour into Hong Kong after fall of Qing Dynasty
1941	Japan attacks and occupies Hong Kong
1945	War with Japan ends
1950s	Chinese refugees flood into Hong Kong following the victory of the CCP over the KMT
1975	Vietnamese "boat people" arrive in Hong Kong and more than 100,000 are accommodated
1984	The Sino-British Joint Declaration agrees on the return of the whole colony of Hong Kong, although the original 99-year lease applied only to the New Territories. China agrees to preserve Hong Kong's capitalist system for at least 50 years after the handover in 1997
1992	Chris Patten appointed as the last governor of Hong Kong
1997	Hong Kong is returned to Chinese rule and Tung Chee-Hwa takes over as Chief Executive of Hong Kong SAR

1

China Today

Within the last 10 years or so, China has changed in so many ways, and it continues to change, almost beyond recognition. In the early 1990's, you had to be aware, and be very wary of the massive numbers of bicycles on the streets of Beijing! The scene nowadays is totally different, the bicycles have declined in numbers to be replaced by motorbikes and cars and the pollution factor has increased considerably.

There are greater numbers of business visitors attracted to the 'honey pot' of China and also a much larger volume of foreign tourists delighting in the treasures and fascinating culture that China has to offer.

The Chinese government is obviously so much aware of this, and their actions in 2000 have deepened structural reform with measures taken to complete transformation from an hitherto closed society to an open market economy led increasingly by the private sector.

No matter how frequently you visit China, you will always be amazed at the continued growth and energy that the Chinese have expanded to improve their country and to establish it as a powerful world economy.

Beijing in the north is the capital and seat of government. It is also a 'grey city' in appearance with its inherited architectural splendours with a strong Russian influence. It has the heritage and sights to attract tourists and visiting businessmen and women, such as The Great Wall of China, The Forbidden Palace, The Temple of Heaven, Tiananmen Square, The Great Hall of The People, plus many, many more.

Shanghai is increasingly becoming the financial centre of China and some pundits predict it will eventually replace Hong Kong as the financial capital, but that is sheer speculation at this stage. It houses the Shanghai Stock Exchange, has two airports, Pudong, which is a major industrial 'city within a city', and is very 'westernised' in both appearance and culture, whilst at the same time maintaining its traditional Chinese appeal.

The international bank, HSBC opened up their first bank in Shanghai in 1865, and have had a continued presence in China since then. Major UK, European and USA companies have established bases in Shanghai and this is testament to their commitment to the future of Shanghai and China.

Another significant industrial corridor is the Pearl River Delta region, which includes Guangzhon, Zhuhai, Shenzhen and other fast-growing industrial cities.

1

Shenzhen is close to the border with Hong Kong and will be the first city you encounter as you travel from Hong Kong either by train, car or on foot across the border from Lo Wu in the New Territories of Hong Kong. The landscape of Shenzhen is dominated by gleaming tower blocks which can clearly be seen from the Hong Kong side and the atmosphere in Shenzhen is very similar to that in Hong Kong, except the roads are not as narrow or as crowded, but nevertheless, still very busy and bustling.

About 1 hour's drive by car northwards is the major city of Guangzhou and before that you will pass close by another city, Dong Guan, which although smaller, is a significant industrial city housing many major industries. If travelling on the Expressway, you cannot avoid noticing the vast numbers of factories positioned close by and the names, nearly all of which are recognisable by business people from around the world.

Guangzhou is the political and economic centre for the Guangdong Province and is said to be the powerhouse and entrepreneurial capital of China! The city was formerly known as Canton and is located in the heart of the Pearl River Delta (PRD), placing it at the apex of a major economic region encompassing Hong Kong, Shenzhen, Zhuhai and Macau.

The city of Guangzhou has a long history as a trading port with a traditionally open attitude towards the outside world. It was said that Guangzhou and Shenzhen, being geographically closer to Hong Kong than to Beijing, came under the "western influence" much earlier than the rest of China by virtue of its access to satellite television. It therefore had more awareness of life outside China long before the population further north and beyond the influence of the satellites beam.

Guangzhou Municipality covers an area of 7,435 square kilometres (approx 2,900 square miles) and has a registered population of about 10 million. Also, it is reputed that Guangzhou is the original home of the majority of Chinese now living overseas. Perhaps that is why there are so many "Cantonese" restaurants outside China !

In addition to these three main "corridors" of industrial growth, other regions of China are now looking to establish themselves as areas of growth and to attract

Foreign Direct Investment (FDI). Examples are Chongqing in the west and Yunnan Province in the south west, both of which are developing fast as economic and cultural centres away from the established "corridors".

The State and Government PRC
In the November 2002 16th Party Congress, the selection of the nine members the Standing Committee of the Politburo of the Chinese Communist Party, was announced.

The Vice President Hu Jintao replaced Jiang Zemin as General-Secretary of the Chinese Communist Party and is expected to take over the Presidency from Jiang Zemin in March 2003.

The other eight members are new to the Politburo:

Wu Bangguo	Vice-Premier
Wen Jiabao	Vice-Premier
Jia Qinglin	former Beijing and Fujian Party Boss
Zeng Qinghong	head of the CCP Secretariat
Huang Ju	former Shanghai Party Boss
Wu Guanzheng	head of CCP Central Discipline Inspection Commission
Li Changchu	former Guangdong Party Secretary
Luo Gan	State Councillor

Population
Establishing the true population figure of China is almost impossible, but current estimates are 1.3 billion. In recent years, China's population has increased by about 15 million annually. With this population, one might think there would be an enormous variety of surnames, but the reverse seems to be the case. At one time, there were reportedly about 12,000 individual surnames in existence in China, but today there are only about 3,000 and the most common of these is Li (pronounced Lee) with almost 90,000,000 sharing this surname.

Most of the population of China reside within the major cities and the eastern seaboard.

1

At the end of 2000, the population of Hong Kong was about 7 million, which equates to a population density of about 6,320 people per square kilometre. Hong Kong has a large foreign population of about 513,200 with the three major contributors coming from Philippines (144,800), Indonesia (63,800) and USA (43,300). The latter being mainly white collar management, and the former blue collar and domestic staff.

Population

In the 1980s, a 'one child per couple' policy was introduced by the Chinese government. This was an endeavour to restrict the nation's burgeoning population explosion.

Official figures issued in 2002 by the Chinese government show there are 117 males for every 100 females in China. This imbalance in the population of the genders was brought about by female infanticide, and selective abortion, following medical scans to determine the sex of the unborn child.

The birth of a boy child was welcomed as it enabled the family line to continue, and, as they grew up, they would work hard on the land and then support their parents in their old age. Boys were useful, whereas the birth of a girl was often referred to as 'spilled water'. However, this policy has had its problems and from the official figures it is easy to deduce that there aren't enough females to go round.

investigating the
potential market

investigating the potential market

An outline of some of the myriad organisations which exist to assist the exporter, along with an assessment of their focus and likely relevance.

The business traveller should, of course, be as well informed as possible before entering a new market. This section acts as a guide to where to find this information. It includes government and private sources in electronic and hardcopy format, and discusses the availability of reliable market and economic information.

Whether you are visiting China or Hong Kong for the first time or making the latest in a series of regular visits, preparation is essential to get the most out of the trip and ensure that your project succeeds. Time, or the lack of it, is more often than not the curse of the business traveller and obtaining the latest information will allow you to plan effectively for your trip, get a clear picture of the market you are entering, identify any trends or opportunities that you can use to your advantage and spot any possible pitfalls. It is equally important to ensure that the information you use is accurate and that you are aware of any possible bias.

The sources below provide a starting point for research on the China and Hong Kong markets. Many of them are free or provide information at very little cost.

2

Contacts for the China Market
British Embassy
11 Guang Hua Lu
Jian Guo Men Wai
Beijing 100600
PRC
❑ Tel: +86 10 6532 1961; fax: +86 10 6532 1937
E-mail: [commercialmail@peking.mail.fco.gov.uk]
Website: [www.britishembassy.org.cn]

British Consulate-General Offices
British Consulate-General
Suite 301, Shanghai Centre
1376 Nanjing Xilu
Shanghai 200040
PRC
❑ Tel: +81 21 6279 7650; fax: +86 21 6279 7651
(Responsible for the provinces of: Municipality of Shanghai, Zhejiang and Jiangsu.)

British Consulate-General
Suite 2802
Metropolitan Tower
68 Zourong Road
Chongqing 40010
PRC
❑ Tel: +86 23 6381 0321; fax: +86 23 6381 0322
(Responsible for Chongqing Municipality and the three
provinces of Sichuan, Yunnan and Guizhou. Principal
cities are Chongqing, Chengdu, Mainyang, Neijiang,
Kunming and Guiyang.)

In Hong Kong
British Consulate-General
1 Supreme Court Road
Hong Kong
❑ Tel: +852 2901 3000; fax: +852 2901 3066
Email: [commercial@britishconsulate.org.hk]

British Consulate-General
7/F Guangdong International Hotel
339 Huang Shi Dong Lu
Guangzhou 510098
PRC
❑ Tel: +86 20 8333 6623; fax: +86 20 8333 6485
(Responsible for the provinces of: Guangdong, Guangxi,
Fujian and Hainan Island.)

Chinese Embassy – London
The Embassy of The People's Republic of China,
49 - 51 Portland Place
London W1N 4JL
❑ Tel: +44 20 7636 9375/5726
Website: [www.chinese-embassy.org.uk]

Consular Section
31 Portland Place
London W1N 3AG
❑ Tel: 020 7632 1430

Commercial Section
1-3 Leinster Gardens
London W2 6DP
❑ Tel: 020 7723 8923

See also the sections on Embassies / Consulates etc in
USA, Australia & Canada for other points of reference.

Ministries and other Government Agencies

UK

The primary British government source for information on overseas markets is **TPUK (Trade Partners UK)**, which brings the export promotion activities of the Department of Trade and Industry (DTI) and Foreign and Commonwealth Office (FCO, into one new organisation. It acts as a first point of contact for market and business information and it produces a suite of publications ranging from introductory guides to China and Hong Kong, to detailed sector analyses. It also offers specialist literature on agency law, etc. and offers a variety of services to small and medium sized companies (SMEs) wanting to break into new markets. These services include specific country seminars and financial support for official trade missions and UK groups attending key exhibitions.

Much of the information held is available on the Trade Partners website at [www.tradepartners.gov.uk]

The contact details for the appropriate TPUK desks are:-

China Unit – TPUK
❑ Tel: +44 20 7215 4230/4827; fax: + 44 20 7215 8797

Hong Kong Unit – TPUK
Tel: + 44 20 7215 4829/4830; fax: + 44 20 7215 8797

Through its Trade Partners UK Information Centre, Trade Partners UK provides information and advice direct to UK business. The Information Centre is a research facility available to exporters and their representatives wishing to undertake their own export market research. It provides access to a comprehensive collection of overseas market information, foreign economic and commercial statistics, trade and telephone directories (as publications, CD-ROMs or Internet databases), mail-order catalogues, and information on multilateral development agencies and the projects and initiatives which they are funding. Access is free. For further information contact:

❑ Tel: +44 20 2175 5444, fax +44 20 7215 4231 or e-mail through its website [www.tradepartners.gov.uk]

2

The Export Marketing Research Service (EMRS) provides a fee-based research service based in the TPUK Information Centre, for exporters and their representatives. These facilities are available through the British Chambers of Commerce at:

❑ BCC: +44 1203 694484 or fax: +44 1203 694690.

Another free source of assistance is Trade Partners UK's Export Promoters now called **Trade Development Advisers**. In 1995 the then Secretary of State for Industry, and subsequently Deputy Prime Minister, Michael Heseltine and his Minister for Trade, Richard Needham, launched an initiative to promote British exports. They proposed to second up to 100 experts from British industry who were specialists either in certain countries or specific disciplines. These Trade Development Advisers (TDAs) are seconded to Trade Partners UK from British industry for a period of up to three years. In a few cases the promoter is an industry specialist (e.g. Environment, Power, etc). TDAs are available to everyone. They are likely to be frequent visitors to their countries of responsibility and will have information relating to opportunities, agents, partners, exhibitions, trade missions, etc. They can generally be found through the Country Desk, or Unit, at Trade Partners UK in Kingsgate House, London, although they may not often be in that office as many either work from home or are attached to one of the regional Trade Partners offices. These TDAs are not only expected to be well-informed but are also likely to be candid about their markets and the opportunities for a particular company. They will usually be able to provide companies with introductions and contacts at the highest level. They have a reporting line directly to the Minister for Trade in the UK. Outside the UK, they work closely with the Commercial Section of the relevant Embassy or Consulate-General.

Since Trade Development Advisers are, through the nature of their secondment, likely to change regularly, it is best to contact the office above to get the current TDA's contact details.

Another key feature of Trade Partners support for the exporting community is the website [www.TradeUK.com], a unique facility for finding new markets overseas, with an internet-based service designed to match British exporters with international opportunities. It is free and accessible to all.

The website: [www.tradeUK.com] can help companies in two ways:-

Firstly, they can register free of charge on the National Exporters Database. On registration, a company's details are placed on the Internet, allowing overseas companies to find them through the database, which is widely advertised abroad. It is also possible to engineer a direct link to companies' own websites. Currently, over 55,000 companies are registered.

Secondly, companies can save time, money and effort by using the Export Sales Leads Service to obtain international sales leads. This service offers hot business leads from Trade Partners UK's global network of staff based in the Commercial Sections of British Embassies and Consulates-General. These leads are matched to company requirements and e-mailed directly to the company. The types of lead are many – specific private sector opportunities, tenders and public sector opportunities, joint-venture and cooperation opportunities and multilateral aid opportunities. It is also possible to access market pointers showing trends around the world, and direct entries from overseas companies. For further information go to [www.tradeuk.com] or phone

❏ Tel: +44 20 7925 7810 or fax +44 20 7925 7770 or e-mail: [export@brightstation.com]

The Business Link network is a series of one-stop shops designed to meet local export and business requirements. All Business Links offer access to an Export Development Counsellor (EDC) who can assist with export related issues.

China and Hong Kong
China Britain Business Council (CBBC)
The CBBC is the Area Advisory Group specifically for the mainland of China and is linked to Trade Partners UK. It is a non-profit body funded by Trade Partners UK and also by industry. Its prime purpose is to promote UK business links with China. Through its network of UK and China-based offices, the CBBC provides expert and practical advice to first-time and experienced UK

exporters on market entry and development. Through local Business Links, it is also now the first point of contact for tailored market information (TMI) reports which are then researched and written to suit your own needs, in co-operation with Trade Partners UK commercial staff located at the appropriate Diplomatic Posts in China.

There is an annual membership fee for joining the CBBC and membership entitles you to six day's free business support in China, free use of the CBBC library for market research, member's workshops where you can meet other members and benefit from their knowledge, inclusion in the CBBC Chinese language Internet directory at low cost, and priority access to Chinese delegations visiting the UK.

CBBC, London
❑ Tel: +44 7828 5176
Website: [www.cbbc.org]

CBBC, Beijing
❑ Tel: 10 6593 6611
E-mail: [cbbcbjmw@public.bta.net.cn]

CBBC, Shanghai
❑ Tel: 27 8577 0989
E-mail: [cbbcsh@online.sh.cn]

Hong Kong Trade Development Council (HKTDC)
The HKTDC is the statutory body responsible for promoting Hong Kong's external trade. It has a 19-member Council comprising representatives of Hong Kong's major business and economic associations and government officials. The Council plans and supervises the HKTDC's global operations, services and promotional activities. In Hong Kong, the Council oversees the operations of one of the Special Administrative Region's (SAR) most important business facilities, the Hong Kong Convention and Exhibition Centre (HKCEC). Trade enquiries can be made directly through the HKTDC 'on-line trade matching service', TDC-Link, which has 48 offices worldwide. They have information on more than 100,000 Hong Kong companies and process in excess of a million trade enquiries worldwide each year, matching suppliers with buyers. For more information, see [http://tdclink.net/]

HKTDC, London
❑ Tel: +44 20 7248 4444
Website: [www.tdctrade.com]

As an adjunct to the Internet services, HKTDC also publishes some 14 product/service magazines and trade directories. With a combined worldwide circulation of more than two million, these publications market Hong Kong products and services effectively and make business sourcing easy for international buyers.

Invest Hong Kong
This is a Hong Kong Government Support Organisation, whose purpose is to provide funding support schemes and programmes and infrastructure support to industries considering investing in Hong Kong. They also offer advice on science and technology resources, productivity and quality, and standards and conformance. Additional help is available for small and medium enterprises (SMEs) and export marketing and export credit facilities.

Invest Hong Kong have desks at the Hong Kong Economic and Trade Offices in New York, San Francisco, Toronto, Brussels, London, Sydney and Tokyo, and assist potential overseas investors in finding business partners and setting up businesses in Hong Kong.

❑ Tel: +852 3107 1000; fax: +852 3107 9007
Website: [www.investhk.gov.hk]

MOFTEC (Ministry of Foreign Trade and Economic Co-operation)
If you are contemplating setting up a company in China, this is the Ministry you must contact for the necessary approvals. These will vary according to the nature of your business and the strength of your local partner.

The HSBC bank suggests purchasing the voluminous book *Starting up a company in China*, which runs to about 600 pages, compiled by MOFTEC and published by Kogan-Page, London. The MOFTEC website is: [www.moftec.gov.cn]

Hong Kong Economic Trade Office – London
❑ Tel: +44 20 7499 9821; fax: +44 20 7409 0647
E-mail: [hk@hketo.co.uk]

UK

Devolution

Partial devolution in the UK, Wales, Scotland and Northern Ireland results in individual countries being responsible for their own programmes, aims, objectives and budgets for the promotion of exports from within their boundaries. For companies in these devolved countries there are considerable benefits and opportunities awaiting them and all governments are receptive and eager to help exporters, be they experienced or new to international business.

England

Business Links (general enquiries)
❑ Tel: +44 345 567765
Website: [www.businessadviceonline.org]

Scotland

Scottish Development International

Tel: +44 141-228 2367
Website: [www.sti.org.uk]

Wales

WalesTrade International (National Assembly for Wales)
❑ Tel: +44 29 2082 5267
Website: [www.walestrade.com]

Northern Ireland

Trade International Northern Ireland
❑ Tel. +44 2890 233233
Website: [www.idbni.co.uk/newstrade/new/index/html]

Your Passport to Export Success

This is a new service offered by Trade Partners UK and exists to advise financially and encourage British businesses to be proactive in exporting. They offer training, planning and on-going support to new and inexperienced exporters. The package or 'toolkit' includes a business health check, mentoring from local export professionals, an individual export plan and development training. Substantial 'matched' funding is available to exporters on implementing an agreed export plan.

Contact:

❑ Tel: 0800 085 4990

Credit Guarantees

Export Credits Guarantee Department (ECGD) is a government department reporting to the Minister for Trade and Industry. The ECGD exists primarily to insure export finance. Typically, a project is structured through the banking system, with ECGD providing a guarantee to the financing bank against default for commercial or political reasons.

One of the most common ways in which ECGD becomes involved with an export is through a line of credit. When a UK bank offers a facility to an overseas bank to enable goods or services to be purchased from the UK, ECGD can insure that risk. The loan facility is used to pay the exporter once the goods have been exported or the service performed. If the borrower fails to repay any part of the loan, the UK bank is covered by the ECGD guarantee. Overseas investment insurance is also available, offering protection for joint-venture or equity investment abroad.

ECGD
PO Box 2200
2 Exchange Tower
Harbour Exchange Square
London E14 9GS
❑ Tel: +44 20 7512 7887
ECGD Helpline: [help@ecgd.gov.uk]

There are a number of private sector companies which offer insurance against payment problems on export contracts. These are generally more suited to manufacturers and trading companies as they offer short-term cover against non payment.

❑ NCM direct: + 44 29 2048 7701
Website: [www.ncm-direct.com]

Trade Indemnity Co Ltd
❑ Tel: +44 20 7512 9333; fax: +44 20 7512 9186

Association of British Insurers
❑ Tel: +44 20 7600 3333;fax: +44 20 7696 8999

Coface UK
❑ Tel: +44 20 7325 7500; fax: +44 20 7325 7699

2

Other UK Ministries

Military Sales

Advice on military sales and equipment can be obtained from a specialist organisation in London, the **Defence Export Sales Organisation** (DESO), part of the Ministry of Defence. This is a very active export service manned by senior diplomats on temporary secondment to DESO. The business is highly specialised, and is handled by the Defence Attachés rather than by the Embassy commercial offices. Defence sales include obvious military hardware and equipment and also takes in the construction of airfields, supply of 4x4 vehicles and uniforms, etc. DESO will also advise on any local political sensitivities.

DESO
Ministry of Defence
Metropole Building
Northumberland Avenue, London WC2N 5BL
❑ Tel: +44 20 7218 9000; fax: +44 20 7807 8307

Education

The task of promoting cultural and educational enterprises and exports is actively undertaken by the **British Council**. The Council, with offices across the UK, is financially self-supporting and is embracing the world of commerce with increasing vigour and imagination. It has officers responsible for exports and for liaison with other government bodies, in particular Trade Partners UK. The British Council has offices in China and Hong Kong. Although still widely associated with its general promotion of British culture and the English language and thus perhaps thought irrelevant to hardcore business, the Council is a leading proponent for the UK education and human resource development sector.

British Council in the UK
❑ Tel: +44 20 7389 4141
Website: [www.britcoun.org or newweb.britcoun.org]

British Council in China (Beijing)
❑ Tel: + 86 10 6501 1903; fax: +86 10 6590 0977

British Council in Hong Kong
Tel: +852 2913 5100; fax: +852 2913 5102
Website: [www.britcouncil.org.hk]

Department for Environment, Food and Rural Affairs

Another Ministry promoting British exports is the Ministry of Agriculture which has been renamed as DEFRA, (Dept for Environment, Food and Rural Affairs) The Export Department in this Ministry has specialised information freely available to businessmen and women. Overseas visits by Ministers and officials accompanied by business people are frequently arranged.

Website: [www.defra.gov.uk]

In general, all UK government offices can be found at [www.open.gov.uk] or use the excellent *Civil Service Yearbook* produced by the Cabinet Office and published by the Stationery Office: ❑ Tel: +44 870 600 5522

The European Commission in China

The European Commission is the executive body – the 'public service' of the European Union, as the EU has no overseas diplomatic representation. The European Commission is represented in China by a delegation in Beijing, established in 1988. The delegation, headed by an Ambassador, has the same diplomatic privileges and immunities afforded to foreign embassies but, unlike commercial or consular sections of embassies, the EC delegation does not deal with trade promotion, consular matters or other issues.

The main purpose of the delegation is to keep the European Commission updated with political, economic and other elements in China and develop bilateral agreements and cooperation with China and EU member states. There are various publications available, free of charge, from the Delegation Information Section. Contact details are: [www.ecd.org.cn]

❑ Tel: +86 10 6532 4443; fax: +86 10 6532 4342

European Union Chamber of Commerce – Beijing
This is another source of European information.
❑ Tel: +86 10 6462 2065; fax: +86 10 6462 2067
Website: [www.euccc.com.cn]

The China-Britain Business Council (CBBC) in London can also offer advice on the maze of Brussels, and much more besides.

2

US

The US State Department and the Department of Commerce provide a wide range of information to US companies or representatives of US companies operating in China and Hong Kong. This is naturally biased towards US business but much of the information is more generally applicable. *The Country Commercial Guides* can be downloaded from the Internet at: [www.state.gov/www/about_state/business/com_guides/index.html]

Specific Information and Support

The specific start point for any US company wishing to consider doing business in China would be to approach their local US Export Assistance Center of the International Trade Administration, the US and Foreign Commercial Service of the US Department of Commerce. (See Appendix Three.)

Australia

The Australian Trade Commission or Austrade is the federal government's export and investment facilitation agency. Austrade provides advice to Australian companies on general export issues, assistance in determining which overseas markets hold potential for their products and aid in building a presence in the market. Through their network of global offices, Austrade can assist with finding potential business partners or agents, prepare publicity material, organise product launches and offer assistance with attending suitable exhibitions. If Austrade cannot help with your specific requirement, they will direct you to an appropriate government or private service which can.

Austrade Online is an enhanced website facility at [www.austrade.gov.au] which provides up-to-date reference points regarding international trade issues and export programmes. Australian companies can also take out a free-of-charge listing within the website allowing inclusion on a searchable database of products and services.

Under their Export Market Development Grant (EMDG) scheme, Austrade may be able to reimburse eligible businesses for part of the export marketing costs they incur.

Canada

With the handover of Hong Kong to China in 1997 looming, and the prospect of a radical change in their way of life under Chinese rule, many of the more affluent residents of Hong Kong decided in the late 1980s and early 1990s to opt for a form of insurance, a 'get out', by moving to Canada and eventually adopting Canadian citizenship. There are strong links with Canada, both in terms of trade and on a personal basis, as many successful businesses were established by people from Hong kong in various parts of Canada particularly in Vancouver and Toronto.

Contacts in China:
Canadian Embassy – Beijing
❑ Tel: +86 10 6532 3536; fax: +86 110 6532 4311

There are Canadian Consulates in Shanghai, Guangzhou and Chongqing; contact details available from the Embassy.

Contact in Hong Kong
Canadian Consulate-General
❑ Tel: +852 2810 4321; fax: +852 2810 6736

Further Sources of Information

The devolved Parliaments in the UK, (ie, Wales, Scotland and Northern Ireland), regional Chambers of Commerce or any trade or professional body to which you belong may be able to provide information on the markets in China and Hong Kong. They may not produce the material themselves, but should have a library where such information is held. These bodies may also offer, for a fee, to research on your behalf. This is more costly, but saves time – to make the most of the service, be specific in defining your research project.

Some of these organisations in the UK have developed good links with both countries through trade missions and also hosting inward missions of visiting businessmen and women.

Chinese Organisations in the UK
China Council for the Promotion of International Trade (CCPIT)
❑ Tel: +44 20 7321 2044; fax: +44 20 7321 2055

2

China National Import Export Commodities Inspection Corp Ltd (CCIC)
❑ Tel: +44 20 8951 3788; fax: +44 20 8951 3787

China National Aerotechnology Import & Export Corp (CATIC)
❑ Tel: +44 20 7586 3854; fax: +44 20 7856 6799

China Aviation Supplies Corp (CASC)
❑ Tel: +44 20 8960 4498 Fax: +44 20 8960 4480

China National Arts & Crafts Import & Export Corp
Wimbledon, London SW19 8ED (contact details not available)

China National Cereals, Oils & Foodstuffs Import & Export Corp
London, EC3N 1LQ (contact details not available)

China National Coal Industry Import & Export Corp
London NW4 4PD (contact details not available)

China Apollo Group Ltd
❑ Tel: +44 20 8640 3212; fax: +44 20 8640 3213

China National Metals & Minerals Import & Export Corp
❑ Tel: +44 20 7411 4012; fax: +44 20 7411 4016

China National Native Produce & Animal By-products Import & Export Corp
❑ Tel: +44 20 8968 4250; fax: +44 20 8960 6196

China National Non-ferrous Metals Import & Export Corp
❑ Tel: +44 20 7495 6593; fax: +44 20 7495 2718

China National Publications Import & Export Corp
❑ Tel: +44 20 8961 9283; fax: +44 20 8961 9282

Sinochem (UK) Ltd
❑ Tel: +44 20 7930 7060; fax: +44 20 7030 4631

ChinaWatch@UK & Associates Ltd
❑ Tel: +44 161 275 6378; fax: +44 161 275 6596
Website: [www.chinawatch.co.uk]

Note: when within the UK, replace +44 with 0, ie, +44 20 becomes 020.

Internet and E-commerce – Hong Kong and China

As you would expect, Hong Kong is well versed in all modern methods of communication and by January 2002, Hong Kong had 409,715 fax lines, more than 2.6 million Internet user accounts, of which nearly 650,000 enjoy broadband access. There are more than 120 Internet service providers in Hong Kong and the on-line revolution is in progress. The Hong Kong Government has launched an electronic service delivery scheme to provide government services over the Internet.

China too is embracing the Internet revolution. The Chinese have an insatiable appetite for information, but there have been strict governmental controls over the use and expansion of the Internet. In the final WTO accession agreement, China agreed to open up its well-protected telecoms sector with significant concessions to mobile phone services including Internet and communications industry. According to official statistics, by end of October 2001 the total number of telephone subscribers had reached 311 million – nearly 24 per cent of the entire population of China and an increase of about 82 million on the previous year. According to the China Internet Network Information Centre (CINIC), at the end of June 2001 there were 26.5 million Internet users in China with 10 million connected PCs. Though figures vary depending on the source, it is a significant growth and reflects the boom in the telecoms sector.

Some useful websites
China

MOFTEC – Ministry of Foreign Trade and Economic Co-operation [www.moftec.gov.cn]

CBBC – China-Britain Business Council [www.cbbc.org]

British Chamber of Commerce in China [www.britaininchina.com]

Hong Kong

HKTDC – Hong Kong Trade Development Council [www.tdctrade.com]

2

Digging Deeper

Once you have an overview of the markets in China and Hong Kong, you may want more detailed economic information or wish to concentrate on your particular sector. This is where the cost of research starts to increase – but you will be very well informed and the risk of unpleasant surprises later on will be much reduced. You will be aware of the trends and the possible effects on your business and therefore able to plan for them.

Economic and Country Guides

Two of the best sources of detailed economic information and analysis are **Dun & Bradstreet** (D&B) and the **Economist Intelligence Unit** (EIU). D & B offer an authoritative, web-based information service which includes data on the intended market. The D&B Country Risk Service delivers comprehensive information sources for evaluating risk and opportunities. Their approach is to combine constant monitoring with an archive service on a wide range of topics. Most companies can qualify for a 14-day free trial period. D&B also offer two excellent business support publications. The first is the *Exporters' Encyclopaedia* – an annual publication that provides information and advice on exporting to almost every country in the world. The second is the *International Risk and Payment Review* – a monthly publication that allows companies to keep up to date on issues affecting the local trading environment.

Dun & Bradstreet
Holmer's Farm Way
High Wycombe
Bucks, HP12 4UL
❑ Tel: +44 1494 422000; fax: +44 1494 422260
Website: [www.dunandbrad.co.uk]

Or

Dun & Bradstreet
899 Eaton Avenue
Bethlehem
PA 18025
USA
❑ Tel +1 800 932 0025; fax +1 610 882 6005

The Economist Intelligence Unit produces a range of quarterly and annual publications which provide a detailed political and economic analysis of China and

Hong Kong. They offer a *Country Report*, an up-to-date monitoring information service, *Country Profile*, which combines historical data and background with current reportage, and a forecast service entitled the Country Risk Service.

EIU
15 Regent Street
London, SW1Y 4LR
❑ Tel: +44 20 7830 1000; fax: +44 20 7830 1023
E-mail: [london@eiu.com]
Website: [www.eiu.com]

Or

The Economist Building
111 West 57th Street
New York, NY 10019
USA
❑ Tel: +1 212 554 0600; fax: +1 212 586 1181

Banks, particularly the larger institutions that operate across the globe, are also a useful source of information, and can usually be accessed through their websites.

Another useful source of market information and news/archive material is **Reuters Business Briefing** – a CD ROM or web-based information service allowing subscribers to search a vast range of information sources for material on virtually any subject matter. It is particularly good at digesting and reproducing news flows from China and Hong Kong and is a good way of following trends as well as tracking down information on individual companies.

Dow Jones Reuters Business Briefing
Reuters Limited
85 Fleet Street
London, EC4P 4AJ
❑ Tel: +44 207 5425043

Trade Associations
Also worth bearing in mind are the **trade associations** – there is one for almost every conceivable industry in the UK. Some of these are large and active in promoting exports. They will assist their members with taking part in trade fairs, can organise seminars and conferences to run concurrently with these events and may target

2

particular countries where they believe the greatest opportunities exist for their members. Those which have been particularly active in China and Hong Kong include:

The Building Centre London
❑ Tel: +44 20 743 1500
Website: [www.buildingcentre.co.uk]

Full lists of all the associations in the UK are available from **CBD Research Ltd** in Kent, who publish a directory in hard copy or in CD-ROM format – full details at www.glen.co.uk Further information is also available from Trade Partners UK.

Seminars and conferences are a good place to meet others associated with China and Hong Kong or with a particular industry. The content of the presentations at such gatherings and the opportunities for networking during the intervals are both important.

Translations
As you would expect, there are a multitude of companies and individuals offering translation services and it is not possible to recommend or suggest any specific organisation. But the TPUK China Unit have a comprehensive list available to suit your specific needs.

Travel advice
Information about flights, visas, etc, is contained in Chapter 3. This section deals with such matters as health concerns and security issues – of which there are none of real consequence in either China or Hong Kong.

UK
The most convenient source of travel advice from the UK is the **Foreign and Commonwealth Office** (FCO) travel advisory service. This can be accessed either by telephone or on-line. It provides succinct information and advice on natural disasters, health concerns, security and political issues. It is more than adequate for most business travellers' needs. Be aware though that it is aimed at a wide audience and is not geared solely towards the business visitor's requirements.

The FCO travel advisory service can be contacted on:

❑ Tel: +44 20 7238 4503/4
Website: [www.fco.gov.uk/travel]
Or on Ceefax on BBC2 page 470

US

The US State Department advice service can be found at: [www.state.gov/travel_warnings.html]. Their reports can sometimes seem alarmist as they are legally obliged to publish any threats to US citizens and their property of which they are aware. Also see [www.usis.egnet.net].

For travel information and advice geared specifically towards the business traveller's needs, you must turn to the private sector. Here there are some good but expensive services which provide more frequently updated reports than the FCO or State Department travel notices. These services tend to be more forward-looking, commenting for instance on the likelihood of further security incidents or the possible deterioration or improvement in the travel environment. They are also usually more frank about a country as they do not have the same political or diplomatic constraints as the FCO or State Department. But the stability of both China and Hong Kong – notwithstanding the situation in some of their neighbours – makes this service unnecessary.

Media

BBC World Service

The BBC World Service broadcasts throughout the world in English and in 43 other languages. An important part of their service deals with developments in British industry, science and technology.

New products and processes developed by British firms are featured prominently in news and other related programmes, with appropriate credit given to the company concerned. All enquiries received at the BBC as a result of the broadcasts are passed on to the companies concerned. The BBC World Service is interested to learn about new processes, innovations, contracts won, etc. and their e-mail address is: [world.business@bbc.co.uk]

It is advisable to take advice before embarking on an advertising programme and the following can be contacted:

Overseas Press and Media Association
Website: [www.opma.co.uk]

2

Voice of America

The Voice of America (VOA) is the international multimedia broadcasting service of the US Government. VOA broadcasts more than 1,000 hours of news, information, educational and cultural programmes every week to an audience of some 94 million worldwide. VOA is broadcast in English and 52 other languages on shortwave, AM and FM radio bands by satellite and on the Internet. In China, you can hear VOA in Mandarin, Cantonese and English. A VOA guide with schedules and frequencies is available from the website: [www.voa.gov] and VOA news is available on: [www.voanews.com]

Keeping up-to-date

An easy way to monitor developments and opportunities in China and Hong Kong is through the press and media for articles and updates on the markets. Both countries receive adequate coverage in the international press and most British and American newspapers and news organisations have correspondents based in the region. The Internet editions of some newspapers and media organisations offer a news service which sends stories on specified subjects to your e-mail address. Others allow you to produce customised pages, which are updated with stories on your chosen subjects. One of the best is CNN's service. [www.cnn.com]

Magazines

China Britain Trade Review
Published by CBBC London

Hong Kong Trader Highlights
Published by Hong Kong TDC, Hong Kong

Overseas Trade
Published by Trade Partners UK, London

China Economic Review
Published by Alain Charles Publishing Ltd

South East Asia Construction
Published by TradeLink Media Pte Ltd, Singapore

International Trade Today
Published by The Institute of Export

Trade International Digest
Published by Croner CCH Group Ltd

Croner is a leading publisher of loose-leaf, regularly updated guidance on international trade with a concentratration on the practicalities of import and export procedures. Recently there has been a focus on in-depth coverage of a specific geographical area, with 2002 seeing the launch of Trading in China and South East Asia. This guide covers 16 countries in the region, and is full of invaluable cultural tips and business advice for companies looking to expand into the area. In addition, Croner's website, [tradeinternational-centre.net,] is a good place to find free Country information, and register for free e-newsletters on your areas of interest. 2002 also saw the re-launch of a monthly subscription magazine **Trade International Digest**.

Croner
145 London Road
Kingston upon Thames
Surrey
KT2 6SR
❑ Tel: +44 20 8547 3333; fax: +44 20 8547 2638
Website: [www.tradeinternational-centre.net]

Encompass
Published as a newsletter by GERLING NCM
Website: [www.gerlimgncm.co.uk]

An excellent specific on-line news and information service is available from China Online:

Website: [www.chinaonline.com]

2

Exhibitions in China

Participating in an exhibition in China for the first time is an experience and you certainly have to be well prepared!

We exhibited at a construction industry related exhibition in Beijing in 1996 It wasn't our first but it was the first time for an Italian company who manufactured equipment and machinery for making concrete. They had taken a lot of trouble and much thought had gone into the design and presentation of their stand. All their main catalogues were neatly displayed on shelves, they had small models of their equipment and plenty of other leaflets, business cards etc all arranged, as one would, for a European exhibition.

The exhibition was formally opened by a prominent Minister at 9.30 am and the morning session was dedicated especially for civil servants and ministerial employees.

The Chinese are renowned for their voracious appetite for acquiring knowledge of all things foreign, especially from the west and within an hour or so, the Italians stand had been wiped clean, just as though it had been attacked by a swarm of locusts !

They had to struggle through the next three and a half days with photocopies of some literature and business cards they had managed to salvage before everything was lost.

The moral therefore is, when participating in an exhibition in China, don't put all your literature, samples, business cards on display at one time. Keep the best catalogues for the visitors to your stand that are from companies important to you. Drip feed the leaflets on to the display and pace yourself for the duration of the exhibition. If you have 'handouts' or 'give away' presents, be aware that if you give to one person, everybody else in the vicinity of the stand will also expect to be given a present.

Once you have participated and survived an exhibition in China, take it from me, the rest of the world is simplicity in itself.

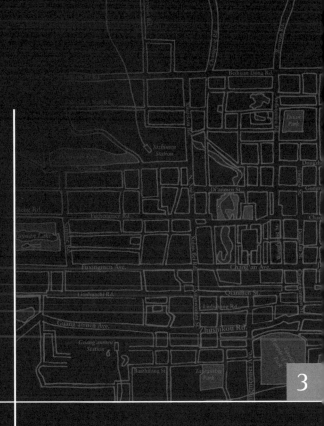

3

getting to China

getting to China

Various considerations in
arranging travel to China and
Hong Kong

Getting to China and Hong Kong

A glance through the travel sections in the press will quickly make it clear how easy it is to get to China and Hong Kong. There are numerous cheap flights, packages and sight-seeing tours on offer. The business visitor, however, has individual requirements and a need for flexibility that rarely fit into the constraints of a package tour.

Check your Passport

As a regular traveller, you will no doubt be aware of the expiry date of your passport. The number of times you have to fill in landing cards for foreign destinations should have the passport number and expiry date firmly implanted into the memory bank.

However, these things have a habit of becoming routine and it is so easy to forget about the dates in the passport when there are so many other, seemingly more important, matters to take care of when travelling on business.

For travelling to Hong Kong and China, your passport should be valid for at least 6 months after your return to your home base is planned. Therefore, if you are planning to be away for 1 month, the expiry date of your passport should be at least 7 months from the date of your outward journey.

Check in areas at airports have witnessed distraut travellers who have been prevented from travelling, either because their passport will expire whilst they are away, or even more commonly, because they have simply picked up the wrong passport, a relatives or similar, in their rush to get to the airport.

Always check, and double check your passport before you embark upon your travels.

3

Even the best laid plans can go awry. Aside from the normal business pressures of re-scheduled meetings, or travel arrangements changing to accommodate a last-minute deal-clinching meeting, typhoons, strikes or lost

Planning

luggage can easily upset your itinerary. It is best to make your own arrangements, and not rely on your travel agent or staff to arrange your flight times. To maximise your time, business flights are best scheduled in the evening – it can make the difference between a half-day wasted and a half-day well spent.Travelling at the weekend or on a holiday gives you a chance to recover from the long journey – especially if it has taken you twelve hours in the air to reach your destination.

Flying time between Hong Kong and Beijing is about three and a half hours, so it is important to plan your trips well in advance. Planning is crucial if you are to maximise the time available for meetings and allow for the inevitability of being entertained by your hosts.

Trade Missions

An important option for the first-time business visitor to China or Hong Kong is to participate in one of the many, regular trade missions to these markets. Advantages of joining a trade mission include pre-arranged flights, hotels, transport, visas, and interpreters. If it is a TPUK-sponsored mission, you will benefit from subvention for participating in the mission, providing you comply with the not-too-onerous conditions, all of which are clearly defined in the introductory information from the organising body, usually a Chamber of Commerce, or an appropriate Trade Association.

Being part of a Trade Mission usually ensures that your group will be in the right place at the right time and it is likely that an evening reception at the British Embassy or Consulate will be included, where you will meet local business people. More often than not, by prior arrangement, you will be able to invite a couple of your own local contacts and the receptions are excellent opportunities for you to impress your guests and meet them socially without necessarily discussing business.

An important element of a Trade Mission is the Briefing Meeting, usually given by a senior member of the Commercial Section at the Embassy or Consulate. This will give you an insight into the country or region you are visiting; it will advise on etiquette, politics, economics, the main players in the market, and possible pitfalls. You will learn from the experts and ask them any questions you like. If you have any problems relating to trade,

Briefing meeting

tariffs, local contacts, etc, just ask the Commercial staff –
they are there to help you. Mixing with veteran
missioners from various business sectors can add
crucially to your knowledge and understanding of the
market you are visiting.

Making Contact

One important benefit of travelling on a Trade Mission
is that some core meetings can be arranged for you
beforehand, by the Commercial Section or mission
organisers. This enables you to at least hit the ground
running on your first visit to the market. If there are
language problems, interpreters can be arranged for
your meetings. From these early meetings, you can
usually gauge the reception and potential for your
business and, more often than not, one seemingly
simple discussion can lead on to other, important
contacts and you will find you scarcely have enough
time to meet them all.

Visas

China

All foreigners intending to travel to China must hold a
valid visa issued by the Chinese Authorities. Business
visas are normally only granted upon receipt of an
official invitation, but tourist visas are more readily
granted. You should allow at least 3 full working days
for processing of the visa. For a business visa, you will
need a completed application form, one passport size
photograph with a company letter signed by a director,
to confirm the reason for your visit, a valid return air
ticket and sufficient company funds to cover costs during
your visit. These should be presented with your passport,
which must be valid for at least 6 months after your
planned departure from China. If travelling from Hong
Kong to China, a tourist visa, which can be used for
business, can be obtained the same day (at a higher cost)
or overnight from the China Travel Service, Peking
Road, Kowloon. For an additional fee, they will also
take a photo of you for the visa application. This is a
good and cost-effective way of getting a last minute visa
for any unexpected trips.

3

Public Holidays in China

Fixed Public Holidays

1-2 January	New Year's Day Holiday
1-3 May	International Labour Day
1-3 October	National Day

Moveable Public Holidays
Chinese New Year

2003	2004
1-3 Feb	22-24 Jan

Public Holidays in Hong Kong

Fixed Public Holidays

1 January	New Year's Day Holiday
1 May	International Labour Day
1 October	National Day
1 July	Hong Kong Special Administrative Region Establishment Day
25 December	Christmas Day
26 December	Boxing Day

Moveable Public Holidays
Chinese New Year

2003	2004
1-3 Feb	22-24 Jan

Ching Ming

2003	2004
5 April	4 April

Good Friday – Easter Monday

2003	2004
18-21 April	9-12 April

Chinese Winter Solstice Festival

2003	2004
22 Dec	22 Dec

Chung Yeung Festival

2003	2004
4 Oct	22 Oct

3

A separate travel permit may be required for remote areas. On departure from China an airport fee of RMB 90 is payable.

Hong Kong

There is an airport departure tax of HK$50, but this is usually included in your ticket. Passengers awaiting and departing on the same day are exempt from departure tax. British passport holders do not require a visa or permit providing their stay does not exceed 6 months.

US citizens travelling to Hong Kong

US citizens can enter Hong Kong for up to three months without a visa, provided they have a passport that is valid for at least one month after the period of intended stay in Hong Kong. Those who wish to stay longer must apply for a visa at least six weeks prior to travel.

Embassy of the People's Republic of China
Room 110
2201 Wisconsin Avenue, NW
Washington DC 20007
❑ Tel: +1 202 338 6688; fax: +1 202 588 9760

3

Timing Your Visit

Timing your visit well to both Hong Kong and China is vital if you are to avoid unnecessary delays and the inefficiencies of bad planning.

Public Holidays
China

There are only 11 official public holidays in China, but even so, it is important to plan your visit around them.

Hong Kong

In Hong Kong they literally have the best of both worlds as they celebrate Chinese public holidays and Christian holidays as well and, in total, have about 16 public holidays a year. This can be extended by the odd day or two depending upon the date of the Lunar New Year in February (see Chapter 4). The 2002 Lunar New Year officially began on Tuesday 12th February with a three day holiday ending on Thursday 14th. Effectively, this turned into a full week's holiday as only the most conscientious turned up for work on the Monday and Friday.

Behind the Yellow Line

Always be prepared for a delay when departing from Beijing Airport and arrive at least a couple of hours before your flight time.

Firstly, when arriving at the departure area by taxi, you will encounter traffic chaos. Then, upon entering the departure hall, you will have to be prepared to queue and jostle for your airport tax voucher, currently priced at RMB 90 for international departures. Buy this before going to the check-in counter. You will then join the queues to check in at the appropriate airline desk, so be prepared for a further wait.

Once you have your boarding ticket, there is a few minutes' walk to the immigration desks and here, you will have to join the snaking queue, having first of all got your Departure Card for Foreigners from the dispenser, which you can complete whilst standing in the queue.

Don't be tempted to join the shorter lines of Group Tours – they have different visas.

After you have successfully negotiated your way from "behind the yellow line" of the immigration desk, a further wait confronts you, as your Departure Tax Voucher is dealt with and you retain the greater portion. You then proceed through an ultra sensitive metal detector arch, where watches, coins, credit cards all seem to cause the alarm to sound, and further delays occur as travellers divest themselves of all such objects into waiting plastic trays.

After all of this, you have entered the open world of the departure lounge and should have just enough time to catch your flight. So be warned, don't leave it until the last minute to arrive at the airport.

Exhibitions

In both Hong Kong and China you will find there is an exhibition of one kind or another on the go almost every week, and hotel rates will fluctuate according to the importance of the event. You may have planned your visit around an exhibition relating to your own business sector, and a visit to the exhibition will be worth a thousand hours of effort. It will give you a chance to see who is in the market and how strong the competition is.

The Hong Kong TDC own the Hong Kong Convention & Exhibition Centre (HKCEC) and they publish a regular list of planned events throughout the year. Website: [www.tdctrade.com]

Another well established organisation is Montgomery International, London, who have been arranging exhibitions around the world for over a century and they can provide a full listing of events in both markets. Their website is [www.montex.co.uk]

Once again check with Trade Partners UK about grants available for participating in exhibitions and whether or not there will be a UK Pavilion featuring UK companies.

China is such a vast, multicultural and diverse country that it would be unwise to commit yourself to any organisation or individual before the market has been fully investigated and explored. Give serious consideration as to whether you would need just the one company to represent you or whether you would benefit from arrangements with different companies in the varying locations. Clearly this decision requires a clear understanding of the strengths and weaknesses of the prospective partner organisations.

Journey Times

By Air

Both destinations are long haul from Europe and America, usually 10–12 hours non stop from Europe to Hong Kong and HK SAR +16 hours from New York.

There are regular daily flights from most major European airports to Beijing, Shanghai and Hong Kong so getting there should never be a problem but seats can be difficult to book around key holiday dates.

3

If you are a regular or frequent flyer, the benefits accrued from points or air miles can be extremely useful, especially in giving economy class passengers access to the Business or First Class Lounge at the terminal. These lounges are more often than not a haven of tranquility, removed from the general mass of humanity in the main terminal, departure lounge area, and the drinks and nibbles are free.

By Train

If your first port of call is Hong Kong and you are planning a trip to either Shenzen or Guangzhou in China, take a train – it is quicker and more interesting.

Make sure you have a visa for China. As mentioned single and multiple-entry visas can be obtained overnight in Hong Kong from the China Travel Service.

The KCR – Kowloon Canton Railway – train terminal is at **Hung Hom**, about a 10 minute taxi ride from lower Nathan Road area in Kowloon. From there, you can board a train that will whisk you, in air conditioned comfort, to Guangzhou in about two and a half hours. You will pass through Immigration on departure and arrival. The station in Guangzhou is conveniently located and good hotels are plentiful.

If travelling to Shenzhen from Hong Kong, the KCR train from Hung Hom, takes 30 minutes to Lo Wu, the last station in the New Territories of Hong Kong and right on the border with mainland China. When you disembark at Lo Wu signs will guide foreigners to the appropriate Immigration desks, on the Hong Kong side, from where you will walk across the river bridge border (which must have kept a barbed wire supplier in business for years) into the Chinese mainland, through the Arrival Immigration desks, and emerge into the hustle and bustle of Shenzhen, where you will be accosted by the taxi drivers. This procedure can take between 30 minutes and 2 hours to complete, depending upon the time of day and number of travellers. If you are accompanied by a Hong Kong local he will be waiting patiently for you as his procedure is faster and formless.

By Car

If you are fortunate enough to make the journey by car from Hong Kong to China, you will find it much faster.

3

From Hong Kong to China

Only cars with dual (Hong Kong and Chinese) number plates are allowed to make the crossing. At the time of going to press there is a limited number of these, but it is increasing weekly.

City Names	
Major Cities	
Beijing	Peking and originally Peiping
Nangjing	formerly Nanking
Chongqing	formerly Chungking
Shenyang	formerly Mukden
Major Ports	
Tianjin	formerly Tientsin
Qingdao	formerly Tsingdao
Lüda	formerly Lü-ta
Guangzhou	formerly Canton

3

Hotels

If you are travelling with a Trade Mission, your hotel booking will be taken care of and you will usually find that the hotel is well located, either close to the Embassy or Consulate or centrally positioned for business.

If travelling to a country for the first time, being ensconced in a central and well known hotel will make it easier for business visitors to find you for that first meeting. Staying in a 4 or 5-star hotel makes a good impression and the standards of 5-star hotels in Hong Kong or Beijing compare favourably with those of other capitals.

China

In China, the main cities are huge and have wide roads and the modern, business class hotels are generally well positioned close to the central business district.

Hong Kong

If making your own travel arrangements and hotel bookings, check with your travel agent about the location of the hotel, especially in Hong Kong. If most of

Rabies

You will see a large number of stray dogs in China, particularly in Shanghai and a high proportion of them are said to have rabies. Avoid all contact with them, in particular avoid being bitten, scratched or even licked. It is recommended that long term travellers or those travelling to remote regions away from medical facilities should seriously consider pre-exposure immunisation to rabies before embarking on their travels.

Chinese Medicine

Throughout the world, the Chinese are famous for their herbal medicines, and in Hong Kong you can find a remedy for most ailments.

Many of the ingredients include tree bark, crushed pearls, insects, reindeer horn, sea horses, a variety of fungi, and snakes, either dead or alive. From the dead snake, extracts of the gall bladder can be drunk and also the fresh snakes blood.

Perhaps the most famous of all Chinese medicinal herbs is Ginseng. This is a root of a plant that has about 30 varieties, its origins vary from Southeast Asia, to North Korea and parts of North America. The bulk of the root resembles ginger in appearance and colour but has very long, fibrous roots flowing from the main stem. It is expensive to buy and the rarest of roots originate from the north east part of China, beyond Shenyang, and prices can reach several hundreds of thousands HK$ an ounce.

In July 1999, the Legislative Council in Hong Kong (the LegCo) passed the Chinese Medicine Ordinance to regulate the practice, use, trading and manufacture of Chinese medicine. Between August – December 2000, Chinese medicine practitioners practising in Hong Kong were invited to apply for registration an order to regulate the storage and labelling of Chinese herbal medicines for the future.

your business is on Hong Kong Island, then go for a hotel located either in Central, Wanchai or Causeway Bay. If your business is in Kowloon, then stay at one of the splendid hotels in Kowloon.

Travel Insurance

Travel insurance is essential and most business travellers will be covered through their own company medical schemes. Most credit cards also offer travel insurance, but this depends on having paid for the air tickets by credit card.

Healthcare

HIV (AIDS) is the obvious health risk and one that now sadly occurs wherever you travel in the world.

Foreign nationals arriving in China are required at Immigration to complete a health declaration card which specifically asks whether you are infected with HIV. If the answer is yes, you may be refused entry. Foreign nationals and students staying for more than six months must produce an HIV antibody test certificate on arrival or undergo an HIV test within 20 days of date of arrival.

AIDS

3

Officially, a UK test certificate is acceptable but the certificate must be notarised and authenticated by the Chinese Embassy in London.

There are no compulsory regulations for entry into Hong Kong or China, but, if in doubt, it is always wise to check with your own health centre before travelling.

Food are obvious sources of contamination and infection but in my experience this is unlikely to be the cause of serious illness in either China or Hong Kong.

What to take

In such a vast country, the climate naturally varies enormously. Throughout the country, the summers can be hot and humid, and in the north the winters can be severe. In the south, Guangzhou and Hong Kong, the winters are mild and the summers hot. Spring weather is unpredictable throughout the country, but the autumn is largely mild and settled.

Be aware that if travelling to Beijing between late November to early March, the temperature ranges from -15°C to -3°C and in summer, from 9°C to 35°C.

Winter temperatures in the northern provinces of the Heilongjiang, Jilin and Liaoning often remain well below 0°C for weeks on end.

Don't forget to pack some casual clothes for the evening or weekend and for women, a shawl or cardigan is recommended when dining out in the evening as the air conditioning in some restaurants can be very cool. Some restaurants do provide shawls, but it is better to be well prepared for this eventuality.

Buying medicines in China and Hong Kong is not a problem at all. Although it is obviously always a good idea to have a small "just in case" pack of aspirin and other basic medicaments.

If you want to take a present, whisky or brandy is usually most acceptable, as is a box of Belgian chocolates, all of which you can buy at the Duty Free on departure.

Travel Agents
There are plenty of travel agents to choose from and the one that serves you best and understands your needs is of course the one to stay with. As in all businesses, they have varying specialties and skills but travel agents I would recommend are:

Portman Travel Ltd
❑ Tel : +44 20 8843 8820
Website: [www.portmantravel.com]

Deansgate World Business Travel
❑ Tel : +44 1732 811822
Website: [www.deansgate.com]

Hourds Travel Ltd
❑ Tel : +44 1785 222522
Website: [www.hourdstravel.com]

4

the ground rules

the ground rules

4

This section takes the reader by
the hand and talks through the
nitty-gritty of everyday life,
from how to get around to how
much to tip the bell-boy.

Personal finances

Currency

Until 1994 there were two forms of money in China, one for the local population called *Renminbi* (RMB), also known as the *Yuan*, and the Foreign Exchange Certificates (FEC) used by foreigners visiting China. Many of the goods available in the shops could only be bought by foreigners using FEC. Thankfully, there is now only one national currency system in place – the RMB. Although the currency notes show *Yuan*, all economic and financial reports will refer to RMB. The RMB is divided into 100 fen; 10 *fen* make 1 *jiao* or *mao*.

When changing your money into RMB it is best to keep your bank receipts which are required for re-exchange on departure.

Be aware of the illegal, black market in currency. The RMB is not fully convertible outside China and it is not worth the risk of being short-changed or passed counterfeit money.

All approved hotels often have facilities for changing foreign currency and travellers cheques into RMB at the same rates as established by Bank of China.

In Hong Kong, however, hotel exchange rates are highly unfavourable so you would be advised to use banks for changing foreign currency into Hong Kong dollars. In Hong Kong the currency unit is the Hong Kong Dollar (HK$). There are 100 cents to 1 HK$.

Credit and Debit Cards

The use of credit cards has made international travel easier, and all major credit cards are accepted in larger shops and hotels.

In Hong Kong using credit cards is almost second nature and it is unlikely that you will encounter any difficulties. Even some market stalls accept cards.

Banks

The Bank of China is pre-eminent in China. The BOC acts as the Central Bank with four large state-owned banks trying to operate under tight restrictions as to what services they can offer, WTO may ultimately change that.

4

Citibank has branches in Beijing, Shanghai and Guangzhou, and HSBC is also prominent having established their first branch in Shanghai in 1865.

The use of ATMs is now common. Look for the CIRRUS /MAESTRO or PLUS emblems displayed by the cash points, as these will allow you to draw local currency. Your own bank will make a small charge for using this service, but the exchange rate will be favourable and you will be able to get cash out of banking hours.

Transport

China

Not long ago the most popular and most widely used form of transport in China was the bicycle, but although cyclists and pedestrians have the right of way, for the businessman taxis are the more common way of getting about.

Taxis are easy to hire and always available around hotels, and are the best way to travel. They are metered but before you start your journey, make sure the meter is on. If the driver makes an excuse about the meter, either that it is broken or it doesn't matter, then open the passenger door, put one leg out and negotiate the fare. You will find that whilst most taxi drivers can't speak English, they seem to have a remarkable ability to understand figures, especially if quoted in US Dollars.

If you are going from your hotel, the best thing is to ask the hotel doorman to tell the driver your destination and agree the rate in advance, but don't forget to tip the doorman for his services (about 5 RMB). When returning from a meeting, ask your host to arrange a taxi for you and to give the driver your destination.

One important tip: never leave the hotel without the hotel name card, in case you get lost or disorientated.

In China, they drive on the right side of the road, or at least they should do! There is a very disconcerting sign on the expressway from Shenzhen to Guangzhou warning drivers of 'reversing cars'. It is not unknown for drivers who overshoot their exit, to reverse down the hard shoulder until they can make a right turn for the exit.

Once off the expressway you will find that motorcycles, bikes, carts, cows and even cars will drive towards you,

4

on your side of the road, to reach a suitable exit, rather than attempt to cross the continuous flow of traffic on to the correct side of the road. Driving in China is not for the faint hearted.

There is also a motorcycle taxi service operating in major cities and you will recognise the drivers by the spare crash helmet and the way they swerve in and out of the traffic, with or without pillion passengers.

Honk Kong

In Hong Kong they drive on the left hand side of the road. The Hong Kong Police are tough on jaywalkers and you should only cross the road at designated crossing points, when the lights are in your favour. You cross at red at your own peril.

You will see an increasing number of dual-plated cars in Hong Kong, especially on Mercedes Benz, BMW and other top-of-the-range models. One will be the standard yellow Hong Kong plate and the other black-on-white, showing the car has been registered in China. The cost of this second Chinese plate is very high, and there is a certain status attached to its display. It allows the car to cross the border from Hong Kong into China, and implies that the owner has significant business dealings, usually in Guangdong Province, which is within easy driving distance of Hong Kong.

Taxis in Hong Kong are highly regulated, and since 1964, licenses have been issued through a public tender system. In 1998, there was a review on taxi policy conducted by the Transport Advisory Committee (TAC), the essence of which was that taxis should provide a personal, door-to-door public transport service.

In Hong Kong, there are about 18,200 licensed taxis, of which 15,250 are urban, red, taxis and the rest green taxis in the New Territories. To improve the communication skills of taxi drivers in both English and Putonghua (Mandarin in addition to their native Cantonese), the Workplace English and Putonghua Programmes were launched at the end of 2000. 50,000 sets of learning kits were distributed and an Internet homepage set up to assist taxi drivers to teach themselves.

If travelling between Kowloon and Hong Kong Island, there is a surcharge for travelling through a tunnel. Taxis

4

cannot stop at bus stops or on yellow lines and seat belts are compulsory. If you need a receipt, most taxi drivers will oblige and some can even print this out from the meter.

Hong Kong Public Transport

Hong Kong has an exceptionally well organised bus system and the double decker buses will be familiar to the UK. There are four franchised operators, the largest and most prominent being Kowloon Motor Bus (KMB) carrying nearly 3 million passengers a day. The fares are competitive and the frequency of service is regular, prompt and reliable.

Buses

Hong Kong has an excellent underground system (MRT), which is continually upgraded and extended.

Hong Kong claims to be the world's busiest container port and in 2000, handled 18.1 million TEUs (twenty foot equivalent units) or in simple terms, 6m (20 foot) shipping containers. According to the statistics, there were 37,680 ocean vessel arrivals, 37,150 departures and a port cargo throughput of 174.6 million tonnes. What you may ask, happened to the 530 vessels that arrived and didn't depart?

4

A useful contact for information on shipping services is the British International Freight Association (BIFA) and their website is: [www.bifa.org]

The longesat railway in the world

Feasibility studies have been commissioned to consider the construction of what would be the longest and the highest railway in the world. Linking Tibet with the rest of China for the first time, the line is planned to run between Lhasa and Golmud in Qinghai Province and construction is start 'as soon as possible', according to government sources. The line is projected to be 1,100 km (about 685 miles) long, of which about 900 km (560 miles) will be at an altitude of more than 4,000 meters (13,000 feet). It is said that more than half of this elevated section of land is permanently frozen.

China Public Transport

One of the most popular rail routes in China is that linking Beijing with Kowloon and in October 2001, following extensive track improvements, the journey time from Beijing to Shenzhen was reduced from 29 to 24 hours. Other, improved routes are from Nanjing to Guangzhou, Zhejiang to Jiangxi, Wuhan to Chengdu and Harbin to Datong. It is said that a top speed of 140 kph (86 mph) is now achievable on certain stretches of line.

A new rail link connecting Pudong International Airport in Shanghai with central Shanghai was launched in 2002. This is a magnetic levitated train project and is the first of its kind to be built for passenger transit anywhere in the world.

Rail

The Chinese Government is putting a lot of emphasis on upgrading, improving and extending the rail network and there are plans for the construction of the largest, urban rail car production facility in China. The Nanjing Puzhen Rolling Stock Works, based in Jiangsu province, will be able to manufacture up to 160 carriages a year and is expected to provide one-third of China's annual rolling stock demand within the next five years.

4

Underground

Beijing and Guangzhou have rapidly expanding Metro systems. The first Shanghai metro was put into operation in 1992. So far, the city has completed 65 kilometres of rail lines. The city now has three more lines under construction and a 23 kilometre line in Yangpu District will start construction soon. River-crossing projects are underway, and the number two Metro line between Puxi and Pudong (east and west of the Huangpu River will necessitate more river crossings.

Underground

Guangdong Province has commissioned a feasibility study on the construction of an underground railway system and high speed light rail transit (LRT) network linking major cities in the prosperous Pearl River Delta region.

Air

Until 1979, air travel in China was a rarity and the preserve of those in government or wealthy businessmen. There was only one airline and both the airspace and airports were under the control of the military. Deng Xiaoping introduced changes to bring much of the air travel under the control of what eventually became the Civil Aviation Administration of China (CAAC). Between 1980 and 1996, more than 40 new airports

Air

were constructed and over 60 existing airports either upgraded or expanded. This expansion continued apace and, between 1996-2000, 17 new airports were built and 33 were further upgraded and improved. The CAAC has been split into seven areas of regional responsibility. There are now 142 airports in China operating civilian flights and under the 10th Five Year Plan, massive new projects are proposed for Western China. The provinces involved are Tibet, Qinghai, Gansu, Ningxia, Shaanxi, Chongqing, Guizhou, Yunnan and Sichuan.

A useful contact for information on airport projects is The British Airports Group, their website: [www.britishairportsgroup.co.uk]

Shipping

After many years of recession in China, the year 2000 saw an increase in shipping volumes and port throughput, with a surge of nearly 33 per cent of international container traffic. The water transport industry is an important part of the Chinese economy, and China aims to provide a reliable and competitive service, exploit further the resources available and build a shipping fleet capable of competing internationally, particularly with Japanese and Korean lines. With China opening up as a world economy, the need for efficient and reliable cargo services for import and export is essential.

There are three main sectors of shipping in China:

International Seafreight: this is dominated by COSCO (China Ocean Shipping Co) who in 2000 carried about 17 million DWT.

Coastal Shipping: the main company is China Shipping Co. In 2000 it carried about 6 million DWT.

River Shipping: the leader here is China Changjiang National Shipping Corporation, which in 2000 carried about 2.26 million DWT.

By the end of 2000, foreign shipping companies had established 21 foreign funded shipping companies and 62 branch companies throughout the main ports in China.

As part of its programme for continuous improvement of services, and also with an eye on the benefits of accession to WTO, the Chinese government announced plans for

4

the strategic development of its main coastal ports. This included making Shanghai an international shipping centre and building container berths at Dalian, Tianjin, Qingdao, Shenzhen and Guangzhou. The plans also include a number of large, deep-draft specialised berths for crude oil, iron ore, etc., as well as improving the infrastructure of old habours and ports by working with city planners to improve the aesthetic appearance of the port facilities and dredging the approaches to increase capacity.

Communications

Postal Services

The domestic postal services in both China and Hong Kong are by and large efficient. In some cities, a same-day service is not uncommon, and you can almost guarantee the overnight service. The international postal service is also efficient. Postage stamps can be bought in hotels.

Couriers

The use of courier services has expanded enormously in recent years as it is usually a fast, efficient and relatively secure method of delivering important documents.

The following companies are well established:

DHL: [www.dhl.co.uk]

Federal: [Express: www.fedex.com]

TNT: [www.tnt.co.uk]

UPS: e-mail: [callcentre@europe.ups.com]

Danzas: [www.aeilogis.com]

Securicor: [www.ssecuricor.com]

Lynx: [www.lynx.co.uk]

E-mail and Internet

Virtually all hotels in China and Hong Kong have e-mail facilities in their business centres. It is wise to check the cost – they can be expensive.

There has been a rapid growth in Internet/cyber cafés and they can be found in all major cities. Illegal, unlicensed Internet cafés have also sprung up in China's major cities, causing significant problems for the

4

authorities. It seems that the Internet has created an addictive cyber-culture. According to *The People's Daily* newspaper in China, the owners of these illegal internet bars are "conniving and profiting from their use by allowing access to pornography, gambling and bad games". They go on to say that they are becoming "electronic drug centres and causing great damage to society."

In June 2002, there was a fire in an illegal Internet café in Beijing in which 24 young people perished, and it was reported that the doors were kept locked to avoid police detection. As a result of the fatal fire, Beijing closed all its Internet cafés pending an official report by the authorities, but licensed Internet cafés in other cities in China continued to function. There are, or were, an estimated 2,200 unlicensed cafés in Beijing but only 200 have official approval. With such a small number of licenses issued, it is not surprising that so many cafés have gone underground.

China's attitude to the Internet has been ambivalent. It cannot deny the massive surge of interest in the information revolution, but regards access to news, comment and information that is available on the Internet as a threat. (see chapter 2)

Hong Kong
Hong Kong has a large number of cyber cafés scattered throughout the main business districts. Costs vary considerably, but the Pacific Coffee Company offer free access to the Internet for the price of a cup of coffee at all their branches.

Like most business travellers, my lap top travels with me everywhere. Using CompuServe and a list of local access numbers I can connect to a local line through my mobile phone, thereby paying only local rates for e-mail.

Telephones
The most expensive, and contentious, item on any hotel bill is often the cost of telephone calls. Use your mobile wherever possible. Reportedly the cost of making international landline calls from China is being reduced in preparation for the opening-up of the network to foreign competition.

4

Domestic calls in China and Hong Kong are inexpensive, and in some cases free, but hotels tend to make a token charge for domestic calls.

Telephone Cards are becoming more common in China and cards are available in denominations ranging from RMB 20 up to RMB 200. In some areas, there are also street stalls from where international calls can be made, at about RMB 20 – 30 per minute.

The use of Credit Cards for making a telephone call from the street in Hong Kong is also a cheap method of making an overseas or domestic call although the 'phone boxes are open sided and you will have to compete with the noise of the constant traffic.

Phone cards are widely available in Hong Kong in denominations of HK$50, HK$100 and HK$250 and are useful for making international calls.

Dialling Codes
The country code for China is 86 followed by 1 for Beijing, 21 for Shanghai, 20 for Guangzhou, and 23 for Chongqing.

The country code for Hong Kong is 852 and for Macau it is 853.

For dialling "back home" from China, you should pre-fix the country code with 108. To call the UK, dial 108 44 and then the area code (without the 0, then the number). From the USA and Canada, dial 108 1 and then the appropriate area code and number. For ATT, dial 108 11, for MCI dial 108 12 and for Sprint dial 108 13.

However, it should be noted that telephone numbers are constantly changing in China as the systems are upgraded and the volume of subscribers increases, so if in doubt or you get a strange sound on the line, check with the hotel switchboard for the up to date information.

From Hong Kong, dial 001 and then for the UK add 44 and to USA/Canada 1, followed by the respective area codes and numbers.

Radio
BBC World Service and Voice of America (VOA) provide good English language coverage, in both China and Hong Kong. Finding their stations on the dial is always a

4

bit hit and miss but you can sometimes discover by accident some other English speaking stations as you scan through the wavebands.

Television

No matter where you are in the world, CNN and BBC World Service programmes will seem to appear on most of the channels available on the TV in your hotel room. There are of course, many other channels to choose from but for up to date international news, these are the most watched.

Freedom of the press does not exist as such and it is said that some foreign observers, trying to establish political trends within the country have learnt to "read between the lines" in newspapers for clues, as they tend to act as a subtle mouthpiece for some government organisations and their policies.

Newspapers

English language daily newspapers are readily available in the hotels in China and Hong Kong although don't expect to find current editions of International Newspapers in the hotel bookshops. They will be at least two days old but if you are out of touch with world events, they can still provide a service to you. The main Chinese newspaper is the Government controlled *People's Daily. The China Daily,* the supporting English-language paper, is published six days of the week, but not on Sundays, and is usually available free of charge, in most hotels in major Chinese cities. Shanghai has two, free, daily newspapers, the *Shanghai Star* and the *Shanghai Talk*, and in Hong Kong, the most popular read is the *South China Morning Post.*

In Hong Kong the English language newspapers are *South China Morning Post* and the *Hong Kong Standard.*

Employment

It is very difficult to get reliable figures on employment in China. Recent figures indicate that the urban registered unemployment rate in China was 3.3 per cent but this does not take into account the number of laid-off workers from State Owned Enterprises (SOEs). After the Communist revolution in 1949 the state assumed the responsibility for providing the iron rice bowl, which ensured that all urban residents were provided with housing, education, healthcare and employment. Technically, therefore, there was no unemployment, although many SOEs had vastly excessive numbers on their payroll. It has been said that China has had no unemployment, just millions of workers sitting idly with nothing to do. The recent reform programmes have obliged SOEs to operate with a greater emphasis of profitability rather than employment , so significant numbers of workers in failing SOEs are being laid off without benefits.

Hong Kong's employment situation, with 3.22 million employed, is much clearer. These are figures released for the year 2000. The employment sectors can be summarised as follows:

Wholesale, retail, import and export trades, 33 per cent

Finance, insurance, real estate and business services, 24 per cent

Community, social and personal services, 14 per cent

Transport storage and communications, 11 per cent

Construction, 10 per cent

Manufacturing, 7 per cent

4

Business Etiquette

To anyone experienced in the ways of overseas business travel, dealing with the Chinese is in no way different from any other people – all that is needed is basic commonsense.

The Chinese are probably more like the British as they tend to be conservative, or reserved, and can be stiff in formal situations. It is important to understand that, within government organisations, most, if not all, of their dealings and contacts would have been monitored by other, so called, government "officials", and their futures determined accordingly. This situation will probably still exist although there has been a significant change in attitudes in recent years, and greater freedom given to those in a position to make a decision.

A formal meeting should always be treated as such and it would be considered impertinent to be familiar. A simple thing to remember is that family names always come first, eg, for Mao Zedong, the family name was Mao, and Deng was the family name for Deng Xiaoping. If in any doubt, always check with the interpreter. There are an increasing number of women in very senior positions in government and business in China so be very cautious about chauvinistic comments, no matter how inoffensive they may seem to you.

Punctuality is of prime importance for meetings in China. Always allow enough time to reach the venue and take into account any potential delays from rush hour traffic. It is always best to be early and wait around for half an hour or so, rather than rush into a meeting, stressed and sweating. If it is your first meeting, you will find that whilst you have had contact with one individual, there will be several other "colleagues" in the meeting as well. These are probably from different departments or organisations, but nevertheless, they may be important contributors for the meeting. It is usual to be introduced first to the most senior person present. An exchange of name (business) cards will follow and, when seated around the table, lay out the name cards in the same order as those seated. Don't be afraid to ask about names once again as they will appreciate that it is impossible for you to remember who they are and laying out the name cards will show that you have serious intentions about the meeting.

A simple, but meaningful, form of politeness with the name card, is to hand and receive each name card with two hands. This can be difficult in practice, as how do you receive a card when both hands are occupied with your own card ? It takes practice, so follow the lead of the Chinese, you will soon get the hang of it and it is a simple but important etiquette.

Always make certain you have plenty, and I mean plenty, of stocks of name cards for visiting either China or Hong Kong, as everyone you meet will want to exchange name cards and if you can have them bilingual, then that will be an advantage. When in a meeting, don't write on the back of a business card, use a separate piece of paper to make notes, as it is frowned upon to deface a business card.

4

Once you are seated for your meeting, tea will automatically follow and will be served on a continuous basis. The cup or mug will sometimes have a lid and when you lift the lid, you will find leaves floating on the surface. A majority of these leaves will eventually fall to the bottom of the cup or mug but, invariably, some will remain as floaters. To avoid a mouthful of leaves, blow gently on the surface of the tea or use the lid to brush the leaves to one side. It goes without saying that the cup or mug will be refilled periodically but don't refuse, just allow it to be filled, and then you choose whether or not to drink the contents.

The host of the meeting will probably take the opportunity for a little light conversation before getting down to business, so be prepared to respond in a similar, courteous manner.

Behaviour at the meeting
As mentioned, there may be other people present from other departments or organisations at the business meeting, so always be prepared for the prospect of having to answer questions that don't actually relate to your own discipline. By this, I mean, that whilst you may have very intimate knowledge about your own sector of business, you might, and probably will, encounter questions to which you have to say, "I will check and come back to you".

4

It really depends on your business and also the extent of your organisation as to whether or not you are able to cope and answer the many diverse questions that will be directed to you. It is advisable to give this serious consideration before embarking on your trip as it can sometimes help to have a colleague with you who can share the pressures of a hard negotiating session.

An important aspect of a meeting with the Chinese is never to be influenced either by appearance or dress. Sometimes, the most important and influential person in the meeting will be the least best dressed. Before starting a meeting, when you have laid out your name cards to correspond with the seating arrangements, ask about their positions and seniority within their organisation and then address your remarks to the most senior person present.

It is most likely that both sides will be using an interpreter. Always direct your answers to the person asking the question, don't look at the interpreter. Speak slowly and in short sentences. Don't use any slang words, keep it simple, precise and to the point. Always brief the interpreter before the meeting as to what you want, or would like, from the meeting. If you have some notes or a simple catalogue or leaflet, give this to the interpreter sometime before the meeting, so that they will have a chance to understand what it is that you are talking about.

It is always wise to have some information about your business already translated and printed in Chinese, as this will be helpful both to your hosts and also to the interpreter.

Also, be aware that if you give a lengthy explanation of an important point but the interpreter translates it into a few words, double check with the interpreter about exactly what has been said, particularly when it comes to figures and percentages. If in doubt, write down the figures in English for both the interpreter and your host to understand.

Be clear about your objectives for the meeting. You have travelled a considerable distance for this meeting and the fact you are there will be appreciated by your hosts but don't forget that when you leave, they will probably go through the same process with another company, and that could be your competitor!

If the meeting becomes heated or engages passion, you must try to remain patient and calm. Don't, under any circumstances threaten to walk out of the meeting – that will cause irreparable damage to you and also any future you might have hoped for in China.

FACE is all important to the Chinese and it is essential to respect this, otherwise your trip will be totally meaningless. Don't demean or call into question the integrity of anyone you are dealing with, no matter how strongly you may feel about the situation you find yourself in as this will surely work against you.

It is not unknown for the Chinese, and let's face it, not just the Chinese, to try to exploit any weak spots or vulnerabilities that may come to the surface, playing off one company against another, sometimes feigning anger

4

or unexpectedly withdrawing, or threatening to walk out, from a meeting. The best defence is always to enter a meeting well prepared and with all the major points and objectives firmly in mind. Be polite and firm but always build in a degree of flexibility; be prepared well in advance to compromise. It is important for both sides not to lose face.

Banquets

One aspect of doing business in China is the hospitality you will receive and it is important to keep a very open mind, and stomach, about dining.

I have often thought that we eat to live, whereas the Chinese, and that goes for Hong Kong as well, live to eat!

Meetings

Visiting a country for the first time is always an interesting experience and likewise, meeting potential clients and partners for the first time, can also be quite daunting.

More often than not, these first encounters are usually at the hotel where you are staying, therefore, you not only have to judge the character of the person you are meeting but also their position in the company.

If you are keen to progress the talks with that client and company, the next meeting should be at their office. That way, you can evaluate their position in the company.

Also, in China, don't go by appearances of manner of dress. Some of the scruffiest individuals I have met have been in a position of high authority. Looks can be very deceiving.

4

Dining, and particularly banquets, can be extremely enjoyable and a valuable opportunity to establish a good rapport and friendship with your Chinese hosts. For the business visitor, banquets are an essential element of doing business in China and should not be considered as an option to be refused. It is likely that very senior people may be present at a banquet who have not previously made an appearance, and if this is the case, then you should be suitably honoured. They may be too senior to be involved in the actual negotiations but key to the approval of the business in hand. The banquet is an opportunity to impress them and also to get a feel for how things are progressing.

The banquet will usually take place in a private room of a restaurant, of which there are usually many such rooms, and you will hear the loud chatter before you pass the rooms as you walk down the corridor to your allotted dining room. The Chinese enjoy themselves when dining and the noise is something you become accustomed to as time passes.

The seating arrangements will be formal. The main guest will be to the right of the chief host, second guest to the host's left with hosts and guests alternating if possible.

On the table will be a "Lazy Susan", a turntable, usually of plate glass with a ball bearing runner underneath, on which will be placed some small dishes of appetisers, usually soft peanuts, and thin slices of raw carrots, cucumbers etc, for nibbling at whilst you settle in to the prospect of a gastronomic delight. The menu will have been prearranged by your hosts, and the dishes will be brought to the table in an order unfamiliar to the western diner. The main dishes will be followed by soup or rice and the final bowl of fresh fruit.

The place setting will usually consist of a small plate and small bowl with a china spoon, chopsticks on a rest and several glasses. There will also be a small bowl and saucer and this will be filled with tea from the moment you are seated and continually replenished throughout the meal. The glasses, of varying sizes will be for beer, water and the smallest, sherry size, for drinking the colourless Chinese grain-based liquor known as *bai jiu*. This drink is extremely potent and it can take some time before the effects are fully felt. Beware of the "toasting" procedure that accompanies *bai jiu* as it is more than likely that one of your hosts will stand up, raise their glass and say to you 'gam bay', the literal translation of which is 'bottoms up'. The contents of the glass are swigged down in one gulp and you are expected to respond. It is not impolite to refuse but the Chinese have a great capacity for drinking like this and if you can participate, it will stand you in good stead and help to develop closer relationships with your hosts. Knowing when to say no, and mean it is important, as being drunk in public is rare in polite society in China, and don't forget, you may have to continue your negotiations the following day and will need a clear head for this purpose.

It is a custom for the host to serve the guest and there are usually communal chopsticks or serving spoons on the table for this purpose. Western guests may be offered cutlery as well as chopsticks. Dexterity with chopsticks is always appreciated, so practice beforehand. The "Lazy Susan" will continually rotate in your direction for you to select dishes of your choice but if you are not certain, or unsure about what is offered, then just leave it on your plate and it will soon be cleared.

It is not considered the done thing but sometimes an enthusiastic host will use his own chopsticks to serve you food. If this happens, you should try, discreetly, not to eat the morsel offered as hepatitis is transmitted in China in this way.

4

Also, if eating from a communal dish of food on the table, it is actually good manners in China only to take food from one side of the dish with your chopsticks. This prevents you from contaminating the dish and if you go to any local restaurant in China or Hong Kong, you will observe diners, seated and eating in this manner. Sometimes they will have a serving spoon, but most of the time, they just stick to their side of the plate or bowl.

Although there are no set courses for the food, the meal is likely to comprise at least 10 or more dishes and will end with either soup, rice, noodles or a simple Chinese dessert and then fruit, usually slices of water melon or similar.

Depending upon the nature, size and importance of the banquet, speeches can sometimes be expected and therefore you must be prepared to respond, as an honoured guest, to the first speech. Keep it short and make the content positive, express your thanks for the business discussions and the dinner, mention the pleasure of meeting senior people (by name and address them individually); restate the objectives of the business relationship, the progress achieved and the obstacles still to be summounted. Finally express confidence that hard work and understanding will result in success. Try not to crack any jokes as these rarely translate well from English into Chinese. One subject that is recognised worldwide is football, or soccer, and the names of famous UK football teams, especially Manchester United, Arsenal or Liverpool don't need translating into any other language. It is customary to end a speech with a toast, so make certain your small glass is fully charged.

A banquet will start promptly and also end abruptly. Don't be offended by this as Chinese do not sit around after a meal as we do in the West. A meal can last up to 2 hours and you have to be guided by your hosts as to when the banquet is over, although it is usually easy to judge, as everybody stands up, bids farewell and leaves.

Informal Meetings
An important function of doing business in China is establishing personal relationships, from which, trust will result. This means getting to know, socially, the people you or your colleagues will be dealing with in the future and hopefully for many years to come.

This is no different from conducting business in most other countries around the world as strong friendships can be forged over a period of time as you get to know your Chinese colleague and these can help to underpin business dealings.

A very important aspect for Chinese people in social relationships is the need to preserve harmony, face and to avoid conflict or confrontation. No matter how strong the bond of friendship between a foreigner and a Chinese person, it is unlikely that a foreigner will be taken into their confidence as they seldom volunteer unpalatable truths for fear of demeaning themselves in the eyes of the foreigner. They would much rather concentrate on emphasising the areas of agreement than causing a foreigner potential discomfort.

You will doubtless come across reference to '*guanxi*' (gwang shee), and this is an important word as it means having 'connections' or 'special relationships', with the ability to get things done in China.

As a foreigner, you will sometimes be referred to as a '*gweiloe*' (gwy low), which is what the Chinese called the

4

very first Westerners to set foot in China, centuries ago. The literal translation is 'ghost like', because the first westerners had blond hair, blue eyes and a very fair complexion, resembling 'ghosts' in the Chinese eyes.

No matter how much you are accepted, you will always be a foreigner and as such, excluded from '*guanxi*' as this is the exclusive domain of the Chinese and, in essence, the true way that a majority of business is conducted in China.

Watches

Watches are seen as an unwelcome present, according to the rules of Feng Shui. If you are given a watch as a gift, obviously accept it the manner in which it is given, thank the person but give them a token coin in return to prevent any bad effects.

Personal relationships exist between school and college mates, having worked together and lived in the same neighbourhood or village or by being related, no matter how tenuous and these relationships can be called upon when favours are needed. Allied to the concept of 'guanxi' is 'houmen' which is the 'back door', the metaphorical key for which is 'guanxi' and considered to be a way of obtaining something by not going through the normal, extremely bureaucratic, procedures.

4

Gay Time

The Foreign and Commonwealth Office (FCO) in London have launched a new section of their travel advice website. It is dedicated exclusively to homosexuals travelling abroad and warns about possible police entrapment and advice against excessive shows of affection in some countries. Britain is the first country to offer such specific advice and it is part of the Government's 'know before you go' campaign. It really is all a question of common sense and respecting the laws of the country, as attitudes towards gay, lesbian, bisexual and trans-gender travellers around the world can be very different to those in the UK.

The website is: [www.fco.gov.uk/knowbeforeyougo]

This system does not imply there is anything corrupt or underhand about the way business is done, it is just an acceptable fact of life in China and one that foreigners will be aware of but will never penetrate.

As a foreigner, it is unlikely you will be asked directly to do any special favours which you could not be expected to fulfill but, if this does occur, you should be alert to the possible motive and implications of being asked and consider taking a step back from the situation.

Once you have formed a friendship in China, it is often long lasting and for good. The Chinese value loyalty and honesty of feelings and will often refer to 'emotions from the heart' as a way of emphasising their affinity with special friends.

Gifts and small souvenirs are often given and you should be prepared for this eventuality. Take something that is significant of your country or region as it is not the gift, but the giving that counts.

4

It is usual to wrap the gift in red paper as this is considered to be a lucky colour. In fact, you will be surrounded by red wherever you travel in China. Green hats and white flowers should never be given as they have unwelcome connotations and clocks should also be avoided as the pronunciation of the words "to give a clock" sounds very similar to a phrase meaning "sending somebody to the grave". Cut crystal glasses and a bottle of whisky or brandy usually go down well.

You never lose sight of the fact that China is still essentially a one party state and still professes Marxism as its ideology. Care should always be taken in expressing opinions that are contrary to official policy and it is important to give due, and full, respect, to this issue and not press your hosts on issues that may seem innocuous to us but very sensitive to them.

For those prepared to make the effort, the rewards in both business and personal terms can be very great but you have to be patient and understanding of an interesting and fascinating culture.

Hotels for China and Hong Kong
The choice is substantial and it is impossible to include them all, but a selection is offered as follows:

Beijing

China World Hotel ★★★★★
located close to all main business areas.

Crown Plaza Hotel ★★★★★
located in Wangfujing shopping area.

Holiday Inn Lido Hotel ★★★★★
situated near the International Exhibition Centre.

Jing Guang New World ★★★★★
located close to the embassy district, business and shopping areas.

Shangri-La Hotel ★★★★★
close to the financial district.

Sheraton Great Wall Hotel ★★★★★
in the diplomatic area and close to commercial centres.

Beijing Movenpick Airport Hotel ★★★★
the best of the airport hotels.

Capital Hotel ★★★★
right in the city centre.

4

Jian Guo Hotel ★★★★
located 4km from the city centre.

Novotel Peace Hotel ★★★
located on Morrison Hill Road.

Songhe Hotel ★★★
near the busy Wangfujing shopping area.

Shanghai

Portman Shangri-La Hotel ★★★★★
centrally located

J.C. Mandarin Hotel ★★★★★
located in the shopping and tourist district.

Jinjiang Tower Hotel ★★★★★
situated in the commercial district.

Hilton Hotel ★★★★★
city centre location and near major commercial & shopping areas.

Peace Hotel ★★★★★
close to the Bund and Huangpu River.

Sofitel Hyland Hotel ★★★★★
located in the famous walking mile with shops, restaurants, etc.

Shanghai Hotel ★★★
in the city centre and close to shops and Jin Au temple.

Guangzhou
China Hotel ★★★★★
located in the city centre.

Dongfang Hotel ★★★★★
located in the city centre and set in large, traditional gardens.

White Swan Hotel ★★★★★
situated on Shamian Island, overlooking the Pearl River.

Garden Hotel ★★★★★
well located for airport and railway station.

Landmark Hotel ★★★★
in the city centre overlooking the Pearl River.

Full details of these hotels, and many others, can be obtained by visiting the website: [www.direct-rooms-china.com]

Hong Kong
The two main locations for hotels are Hong Kong Island and Kowloon.

For the hotels listed, E = economy price, M = medium price and L = luxury price categories.

Hong Kong Island
Causeway Bay

Metropark Hotel – E

Regal Hong Kong Hotel – L

Rosedale on the Park – L

Central
Island Shangri-La Hong Kong Hotel – L

Mandarin Oriental – L

JW Marriott Hotel – L

The Ritz Carlton Hotel – L

Happy Valley
Emperor (Happy Valley) Hotel – M

North Point
Ibis North Point Hotel – E

Newton Hotel – E

City Garden Hotel – E

Wanchai
Novotel Century HK Hotel – M

Grand Hyatt HK Hotel – L

Harbour View International House – E

Renaissance Harbour View Hotel – L

The Warney Hotel – E

The Charterhouse Hotel – E

Of these locations, Causeway Bay, Wanchai and Central are the best situated for business travellers. There is good access to the MTR from all locations mentioned.

Kowloon
Tsim Sha Tsui and Tsim Sha Tsui East

The Peninsula HK – L

Kowloon Shangri-La Hotel – L

The Sheraton HK Hotel – L

Hyatt Regency HK Hotel – L

The Royal Garden Hotel – L

Hotel Inter-Continental HK – L

Great Eagle Hotel – L

New World Renaissance Hotel – M

Holiday Inn Golden Mile Hotel – M

Kowloon Hotel – E

BP International House (The Boys Scouts) – E

Empire Kowloon – E

Guangdong Hotel – E

There are many websites available giving full details, and much more, of the hotels and deals available. Try:
[www.hongkonghotels.net]

4

Public Holidays

The Chinese have the Lunar Calendar and in Hong Kong they have the Gregorian Calendar but also observe the Lunar dates as well, so they get the best of both worlds when it comes to public holidays!

The public holidays are:

Lunar New Year's Day (1st Feb 2003) – HK and China

Second Day of the Lunar New Year (31st Jan 2003 ** note) – HK and China

Third Day of the Lunar New Year (3rd Feb 2003) – HK and China

International Women's Day – (March) – China only

Ching Ming Festival – (5th April 2003) – HK only

Good Friday – (18th April 2003) – HK only

The day following Good Friday – (19th April 2003) – HK only

Easter Monday – (21st April 2003) – HK only

Labour Day – (1st May 2003) – HK & China

Chinese Youth Day – (early May 2003) – China only

The Buddha's Birthday – (8th May 2003) – HK only

International Children's Day – (1st June 2003) – China only

Tuen Ng Festival – (4th June 2003) – HK only

Hong Kong SAR Establishment Day – (1st July 2003) – HK only

Founding of the Chinese Communist Party (CCP) – (1st July 2003) – China only

Army Day – (1st August 2003) – China only

The day following Chinese Mid-Autumn Festival – (12th September 2003) – HK only

National Day – (1st October 2003) – HK & China

National Day – (2nd October 2003) – China only

Chung Yeung Festival – (4th October 2003) – HK only

Christmas Day – (25th December 2003) – HK only

The first weekday after Christmas – (26th December 2003)

** Note

"As the second day of the Lunar New Year for 2003 falls on a Sunday, the day preceding the Lunar New Year's Day will be designated as an additional general holiday", according to a HK government spokesman.
See also Chapter 3 page 68.

Travellers' Tips

Tipping

When dining out in larger Chinese restaurants in either China or Hong Kong, you will be met and taken to your table by a hostess. Once seated, the first service to appear will be tea and it will keep on coming, right throughout the meal. If your host is a local, leave it for him to choose the dishes as there will be much discussion over a seemingly simple function but it involves how the food is cooked, how fresh it is, sauces, etc, and is usually conducted at a relatively high decibel level.

The service will seem abrupt and sometimes verging on being rude but you have to make allowances for varying cultures. Don't be put off by this attitude, as the service you receive will be good, efficient and effective. In most restaurants, the food will be brought to the table by a kitchen maid and she will stand, quite obediently, by your table waiting for a waiter or waitress to place the dishes on the table, or Lazy Susan, and if soup is on the menu, your bowls will be filled, and refilled automatically, as required.

Your tea will be replenished, your beer glass filled, the plates and bowls replaced on a regular basis and all your needs attended to in a very calm and efficient manner by staff who earn the minimum of wages. A service charge will always be included in your bill and if you approve of the service you have received, then an extra tip will always be appreciated.

Disabled Traveller

The needs of disabled travellers in China have not really been recognised until recent times but even so, there is little accessibility on public transport and some institutions, although most modern offices and hotels have made provision for the needs of visitors with disabilities.

4

China is a country of steps, crowded streets and unpleasant lavatories. Airlines and airports have made some efforts to improve their facilities, and wheelchairs can be provided, when necessary.

The best advice is to contact your travel agent, embassy or consulate for more information on the provisions for the disabled traveller.

Lavatories

It may seem like a very basic subject, but when you are 7 or 8 hours ahead of BST or GMT, it takes a while for your bodily functions to catch up, and to readjust, not only to the time difference, but also the radical change in food, drink and ambience. Be prepared, are the watchwords, travel with a small pack of tissues or a supply of your own toilet paper and keep in mind the proximity of any good class hotels, as they can be very useful in the event of an emergency.

Outside of hotels, public toilets are usually quite dreadful and it really is best to avoid them, unless you are totally desperate. If you have to use a public toilet, be prepared for a hole in the ground, no privacy and also a total lack of accuracy. Sometimes, washing facilities are provided, for a few *fen*, but in a majority of cases, such luxuries don't exist.

The facilities in restaurants can be slightly better, especially in establishments that cater for foreigners, but don't forget to take your own toilet paper or pack of tissues, as a simple thing like that is invariably in short supply, or non-existent.

4

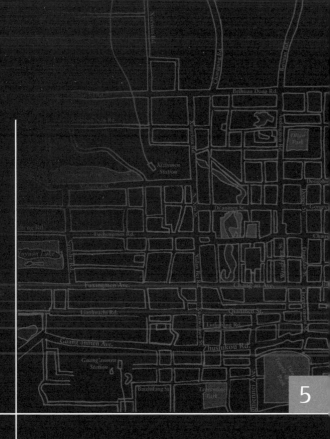

5

getting down to business

getting down to business

This chapter provides elementory guidance on the basic etiquette of business, and also contains details of useful local organizations who can assist with the more complicated requirements of business transactions.

China should not be seen as one market, but a collection of several markets.

There are two types of exporting. One is the planned structure involving large investment, multilingual staff, offices and manufacturing plants located sometimes in exotic, sometimes in dreadful places – but out there, doing business, as a flagship for UK enterprise. The other, is what I call accidental export, where companies produce goods that have an export market, but for whatever reason – intransigence, lack of awareness and foresight on the part of the management – wait for overseas enquiries to come to them.

There is a well known adage in the business of exporting, 'do you make what you sell or do you sell what you make?' You must adapt according to he market. See chapter 2 for the best way to approach and evaluate the potential market.

No Problem

This is one of those phrases that is universal, and it will be regularly heard in both China and Hong Kong. In Mandarin, ''no problem'' translates phonetically as ''may won tee'' and in Cantonese, as ''mo man tai''. I can guarantee you will hear these words in everyday conversation, particularly in Hong Kong.

5

Why China?
The crash of Asian economies in 1997 had a serious knock-on affect on many economies but China maintained its position as a powerful magnet for foreign investors. China is considered to be the most cost-effective place in the world to set up a manufacturing facility and it is reported that Japanese and USA companies are cutting back their domestic investments in favour of expanding heavily into China.

In 2001, China had a GDP growth of 7.3 per cent and this was above the government's 7 per cent target. Domestic growth was the driver and this demand was sufficient to offset the sharp declines in external growth.

One reason for this is China has a population of 1.3 billion domestic customers. Another factor is that China is opening up its borders, making it easier to invest, and gives companies established there a competitive edge in world markets.

The government's overriding policy objective is economic growth and the annual average target set for the 10th Five Year Plan, 2001–2005, is 7 per cent and is seen as the minimum growth rate for maintaining China's social and economic stability over that period.

The RMB currency is likely to remain closely linked to the US dollar in the short term, and there is currently little pressure on the exchange rate.

Feng Shui

Feng Shui is the ancient art of harnessing the heavens and the earth to bring health, wealth and good fortune by tuning into the environment, seasonal changes, tides and vibrations of nature.

It is also a very significant source of revenue for its practitioners as Feng Shui is used by architects and construction companies, on projects ranging from office blocks, banks, private homes, shopping malls and new town developments.

Feng means "wind' and Shui "water" and these are very significant and important factors for the Chinese and their own living styles.

Establishing a Presence

Much depends on the nature of your business and the manner in which you want to enter the market in China and Hong Kong. The first things to ask yourself are:-

● Am I prepared for a long haul?

● How long am I, or my shareholders, prepared to wait before we see any financial return on the investment?

● Can we afford to invest in China or Hong Kong without any adverse effect on our cash flow and current position in other markets?

● Can we afford not to invest in China?

● How much will it cost us to get out of any

arrangement, joint venture or collaboration, if we fall out of favour or there are difficulties with our Chinese partners?

● What about Intellectual Property Rights and Trade Marks?

● Are we well protected against any infringement or pirating of products in China?

There are many ways to setting up a business in China and they include:

The Cheap Route
Appointing a representative company
This is the simplest method and will give you the least exposure to problems involving a simple agreement or understanding for a person or company to represent you on the market. They will agree to sell your product based on your lowest price, to which they add a margin for themselves. Usually, the client will buy the goods or services directly from you, against the agreed payment terms, and you transfer the difference, as commission, to the representative's account, when you are paid. Always work on the basis of paying when paid, that is important!

Working with an agent
This works on the same basis as above but the agent will fund the transaction and in, that way, disguise exactly what his margin is on the deal. You have to make certain the agent has the funds to cover the deal and also to pay you on the agreed terms, i.e. trade on the basis of letter of credit terms.

Appointing a distributor
If your product is a relatively fast moving commodity, then a distributor will keep your product, or products, in stock for re-sale to the market through their own business network. Secure payment terms are important as some of their clients will be given extended credit, so you could find yourself in a pay when paid situation from your distributor. This is not uncommon and, obviously, commercial acumen is vital to avoid financial embarrassment.

These arrangements are relatively cheap to operate as they require little or no actual financial investment on

5

your part, except of course the cost of regular visits to the market to keep track of what is happening and how you can improve your market share. Local management will appreciate these visits and should benefit from your input. You will also acquire a more intimate knowledge of the market as time progresses and you can adapt your own methods and techniques to good advantage.

The More Expensive Route
Setting up a joint venture

A Foreign Invested Enterprise (FIE) can set up as a JV or a Wholly Foreign Owned Enterprise (WFOE) and historically, many FIEs were set up as JVs and for certain industries, MOFTEC approval would only be granted to JVs.

There are two types of JVs, an Equity Joint Venture (EJV) and a Contractual or Co-operative Joint Venture (CJV). An EJV is a limited liability corporation and a legal entity in China. Partners jointly operate the EJV, share the risks, profits and losses according to their share of the equity. Foreign partners are allowed to repatriate their share but don't forget, the RMB is not, as yet, a fully convertible currency.

A CJV involves a different division of responsibilities from an EJV. Under a CJV, the Chinese partner will provide the JV with non-liquid assets, eg, land, energy resources, labour, usable buildings, machinery and facilities, etc. The foreign partners will provide the capital, technology, specialised equipment, materials, etc. A CJV contract is signed, detailing the rights and obligations of each party and also the distribution of the CJV's products, revenues and profits. The profits are shared in accordance with the proportions stipulated in the contract.

FIE is restricted to selling the goods it produces; it cannot sell goods produced by other FIEs although, as a result of entry into WTO, these restrictions are to be lifted gradually over the next few years.

Many JVs have not worked out successfully, principally due to the failure of each party to recognise that, despite frequent professions of mutual activity, they have their own agendas and objectives.

In some extreme cases, the unrest between the JV parties has resulted in the Chinese partner registering complaints to either the tax authority of other ministries about an alleged violation by the foreign investor. Because of these difficulties FIEs are increasingly seeking to convert JVs to WFOEs.

Establishing your own company (WFOE)
This is, as the title describes, an enterprise established on Chinese soil, whose entire capital is invested by foreign concerns. WFOEs are subject to Chinese Law and are expected to play an active role in developing China's economy whilst generating unusually high profits which will yield taxation revenue for the government. This is not for the faint-hearted or SME type company.

WFOEs

China Holding Company (CHC)
Setting up a CHC is an expensive proposition and there are only a handful of multinational companies willing, or capable of making the investment. To establish a CHC requires a minimum registered capital of US$30 million, and this has to be fully paid up within two years. There are also significant tax and operational burdens but nevertheless, the number of companies interested in CHC is growing. Some of the most well known brand names have CHCs, including Caterpillar, BASF, GM, IBM Microsoft, Nestlé, Sony, General Electric, Coca Cola and Ericsson. Nine out of 14 semi-conductor firms in China have established a CHC and they include Toshiba, Sanyo, Samsung, Motorola, NEC and Philips. Almost 90 per cent of CHCs are located either in Beijing or Shanghai. CHCs are granted approval by MOFTEC and whilst there are constraints, such as tax and operational burdens, there are many ways for multinational companies to benefit and profit from this system. It is said that having a CHC puts a company in an exclusive club and this can have obvious advantages in China.

5

Since August 1999, a new, Super Holding Company (SHC) system has been permitted, allowing some qualifying CHCs to restructure their operations. The regulations and requirements are complicated and expert advice should be sought.

Setting up a Joint Development (JD)
This term is normally applied to companies involved in joint exploration for off-shore hydrocarbons – oil companies. The terms and conditions of this venture are complex and involve different stages of development with significant risks from the outset.

JD

Establishing a Compensation Trade (Counter Trade) Deal

This is another complicated venture which involves the Chinese partner providing factory buildings and labour with the foreign partner supplying production equipment, technology, supervisory personnel and possibly some of the raw materials not otherwise available in China. The repayment to the foreign investor is a complicated procedure and very specific advice should be sought if you are contemplating such a venture.

Buying a local company and incorporating their operations with yours

This is something to consider, especially if you locate a private sector company. Buying or investing in a public sector company is possible, but will be a very difficult deal to complete.

Leasing Deal

Foreign companies provide the Chinese leasee with specific equipment, machinery or other services, either directly or through leasing service corporations or leasing agents. The agreement includes scheduled re-payments as instalments and the foreign company, or its agent, is responsible for dealing with the customs formalities.

A useful website is: [www.pwcglobal.com/uk/ibn]

Expert Advice

With the financial collapse of companies such as Enron, ITV Digital, WorldCom, Vivendi, etc, in 2002, and suspicion hanging over the accounting procedures of many other multi-national companies around the world, the role of the 'expert', has invariably been called into question.

Western companies continue to make big mistakes, and the bigger the company, the greater the publicity and ultimate impact on its dealings, investors and position on the stock market. Establishing a business in China has to be a long haul procedure, and those companies who plan, research and then embark upon a long term view, will eventually find the business opportunities and returns of realistic profits expected when they first set out on the journey to discover China.

There are some pundits, 'experts', who see China as a false dream, and declare that the margins and rates of

5

return on investments are low because of over-regulation of the business system by the Chinese authorities.

However, Chinese rules and regulations are not necessarily as extreme as they can be in the EU, and if you know your market and business, have trust in your partner and think long term, you will receive a fair return for your investment. This is, of course, on the assumption that your product sells and the business is effectively managed.

Interpreter

As has been mentioned, the Chinese have two main languages, Mandarin & Cantonese. Because the characters are the same, they can write to each other but have great difficulty communicating orally.

In 1996, we had a stand at an exhibition in Beijing and it was arranged in conjunction with our representative company, based in Hong Kong. The manager from Hong Kong, a Cantonese speaker, and I, met at the appointed hotel in Beijing on the Sunday before the exhibition and he announced he had arranged for an interpreter to be with us, on the stand, for the duration of the exhibition. I thought this was a good idea as my Mandarin, and Cantonese, was non-existent but I was mistaken, the interpreter was for him, to communicate with the Mandarin speakers !

He had arranged to meet the interpreter at the hotel on Sunday afternoon and at the appointed hour, we were both sitting in the hotel reception area, when a delightful, young and attractive Chinese lady was directed to us by the concierge. As we stood up, she introduced herself by her adopted Christian name of Cathy and said she would be our "interrupter" for the next few days. It was a memorable exhibition.

5

Another argument against investment is that it is very difficult to make money in China and it is wrong to think of Chinese streets being paved with gold.

A counter to this argument is to explore and understand why some high profile, and less well known, organisations have failed in China. In simplistic terms, the reasons are generally a lack of planning, unreasonably high expectations at the outset, a 'quick fix' solution to solving their own domestic problems by investing overseas, inexperienced and insensitive expatriate management, with an over-superior attitude. Plus an over reliance on the influences of *guanxi* and an immature understanding of the Chinese characteristics and market place.

The market potential for China should not be underestimated. China is growing and growing fast, and you have to be flexible to be able to keep pace with its development, and if you don't, someone else will fill your space, and probably be successful.

With the right attitude, ideas, sound knowledge of its culture and desire to succeed, success and profits are possible. A major, multi-national company is reported to have declared that they were in Beijing because, for them, it is an ideal base from which to produce and service not just China, but the whole of their South East Asia markets. They were not there just because it provides cheap labour but, geographically, because it is ideally suited and enabled them to be cost effective and profitable.

A further, fundamental reason is that raw materials are readily available, although sometimes not of highest quality, but in China – and in life in general – everything is possible with a little effort, and the infrastructure for local supply to meet international standards is improving on an almost daily basis.

It is an interesting fact that, in the 21st century, thousands of young Chinese students are being accommodated in expensive British public schools, paid for by their parents' private savings.

In a majority of cases, those private savings, and disposable income, would be generated from earnings through collaboration with foreign investors. This in itself creates a greater need for self advancement, not only for the parent, but also for future generations of Chinese entering business, who will become the captains of industry in conjunction with the accession of foreign partners.

Even the process of thinking about investing in China will lead you down the route of considering expert advice. There are plenty of firms around, all ready and willing to take money off you for their sound advice, but the places to start will surely be through your own country embassy or consulate, Trade Partners UK – China Unit or the CBBC, all of whose contact details have previously been given in chapter 2.

Despite all its limitations, obstacles and apparent hindrances, the conclusion has to be that China is a good market, provided you move in with your eyes wide open.

Useful Considerations

World Trade Organisation (WTO)

After a 15 year guest China finally joined the WTO in December 2001. The consequence of this acession will be profound and will affect all aspects of Chinese economic life. Transparency and accountability will be brought in line with international standards, subsidies will be withdrawn and tariffs and other protective devices will be lowered. All of these will impose immense pressure as China's somewhat fragile social structure , with the huge agricultural sector facing competition from cheaper imports and SOEs having to close due to the removal of non-performingloan facilities. The collapse of the 'iron rice bowl' culture has already resulted in mass lay-offs in 'rust belt' industries in Manchuria and the potential for social unrest remains significant.

5

As China moves closer towards adopting international practices then Hong Kong's advantages of the rule of law and the international recognition of its financial system may become less evident.

The advantages of being part of the WTO are:

● Lower tariffs on a wide range of goods.

● Import quotas to be phased out.

● 'National Treatment' for foreign companies.

● A regulated dispute settlement mechanism.

The disadvantages of WTO membership include:

● As tariffs and customs duties are reduced on imported products, FIEs producing in China will face threats, not only from domestic companies, but also from firms producing in other, cheap-labour countries in the Far East region.

- Under WTO, China may have to remove some, or possibly all, of its tax incentive schemes which were originally designed to attract foreign direct investment (FDI).

Local knowledge

The practice of the State government and its various ministries is to issue many regulations which are then followd by 'Guidelines for the implementation of...' As each province and municipality operates with considerable autonamy and independence from Beijing so these regulations are interpreted in many different ways. Priority will invariably be given to the interpretation which gives greatest benefit or least disadvantage to the province/muniipality itself.

The success of any project will be heavily dependant upon the local interpretation and implementation of such regulation insofar as they will affect your chosen form of business operation.

The Hong Kong Route

An other way of doing business with China is through Hong Kong. The benefits of this approach are:

- There are no barriers to market entry, and English Common Law is the basis of commercial contract law.

- British Standards or British-compatible standards are widely used in engineering and construction specifications.

- The Hong Kong business scene is fast moving and highly entrepreneurial.

- Money from Hong Kong can be freely repatriated and you will be dealing with English-speaking managers who will be running the business on your behalf, unless you employ your own nationality staff to look after your interests.

The downside is that you will never be totally in charge or control of the dealings between Hong Kong and China and will have to rely entirely upon the honesty of your partner.

Hong Kong continues to be the largest external investor in the mainland of China. This investment has been concentrated mainly in Guangdong province, where

5

industrial investment, primarily for production for export, still predominates. Entrepreneurial Hong Kong businessmen have extended the scope of their investments to include residential developments, hotels and tourist related projects, retail trade, infrastructural development and multi-various other opportunities.

Many of these businessmen, or their families, originate from the Guangdong region, and they enjoy returning to their roots, displaying how well they have done in Hong Kong, and re-investing in their original community.

ChinaLink

There are at least three excellent organisations who can advise, provide information and support in your quest to establish business in China:

Trade Partners UK – China Unit: [www.tradepartners.gov.uk]

China Britain Business Council (CBBC): www.cbbc.org

ChinaLink (Liverpool Chamber of Commerce & Industry): [www.chinalink.org.uk]

ChinaLink have an office in Shanghai but contact should be through the Liverpool, UK, office.

ChinaLink in particular has special expertise in assisting companies to explore and set up in China but all three will be able to provide you with information to set you off on the right route.

5

the longest journey starts with a single step

The City of Liverpool is twinned with the City of Shanghai and Liverpool has the oldest community of Chinese residents in Europe, reputedly dating back to the 19th century, the community that is, not the age of the residents! Liverpool was a major shipping and trading port. It also has an excellent "China Town" area of restaurants.

Location

Choosing the right partner is one obvious prerequisite to success in China but choosing the right location is equally important. China is such an enormous landmass that geographical location, access to port facilities, road systems, airports, raw material suppliers, specialised labour, etc, are all important factors when deciding where to set out your stall.

Each province in China will be courting you, offering you incentives to locate in their region; even consulates will be keen to encourage you to their area of responsibility. The pressure will be significant and you will have to consider, most seriously, the city that suits you best and that is right for your business.

Eastern Promise

The eastern coastal region is extremely well developed and sophisticated in what it has to offer foreign investors and the process of establishing businesses, particularly in Shanghai and Tianjin, is relatively simple.

The 'Shanghai Vision', is for Shanghai to become a world class city by 2015, to generate 15 per cent GDP by the same year and to be the new financial centre of the whole region and also the new ICT capital.

The vision aims for six pillar industries to be well established:

Information and IT, Financial Services. Goods Distribution, Automobile Manufacture, Real Estate, Complete Sets of Equipment.

The last item means that all the component products will be produced in China and assembled to create the complete piece of equipment or machinery. They will not have to rely upon imported components, no matter how small, or technical.

However, to keep us in touch with reality, it should be noted that in 2002, 8 per cent of the population of Shanghai still do not have access to cold running water.

Go West

Much emphasis is being placed on the western region of China and its development remains a top priority for the Chinese government. At the end of 2000, the State

5

Council announced the four key pillars of its strategy, aimed at creating a more attractive environment for investors:

- Increased capital investment in infrastructure development
- Favourable investment incentives
- Widened scope for foreign investment
- Investment in people.

Pyjama game

A Shanghai newspaper published an urgent plea during August 2002, requesting residents of the city to stop wearing pyjamas on the streets. Shanghai was bidding to host the World Exposition in 2010 and the conservative daily newspaper Wen Hui Bao, called the habit "coarse and uncivilised", but this form of attire has become part of the landscape of Shanghai, causing further castigation from the newspaper, referring to the fact it is "spoiling the view of an international city."

It seems some women even choose their nightgowns with an eye on turning the sidewalk into a catwalk for an impromptu fashion show, and according to a report from a leading fashion store, some customers want beautiful pyjamas which are suitable to wear outside as well as at night. This certainly adds to the character of an already fashionable city.

5

Chongqing is situated on the upper reaches of the mighty Yangtze River and is the only Municipality in Southwest China that reports directly to the central government.

Chongqing has a total population of more than 30 million and is a traditional commodity exchange centre. Over 50 airlines serve the international airport. The rail network is in need of improvement but the facilities are being expanded. The Port of Chongqing is also being developed to handle larger volumes of container traffic.

Heavy industry is an important factor in Chongqing's economy and accounts for more than 60 per cent of its output. Pillar industries include auto and motorcycle production, chemicals and pharmaceuticals, food and related products, construction materials and tourism.

Foreign-funded enterprises have become a new growth area in the economy of Chongqing and nearly 30 of the world's top 500 industrial enterprises have invested in there.

The areas of specific interest for future foreign investment are:

● Construction and infrastructure, ie, consultancy and the supply of specialised machinery and technical equipment.

● The development of the Light Rail and Metro system in Chongqing.

● Oil and gas sector.

● Water treatment technology.

● Construction materials.

The Deep South

Guangdong is China's fifth largest province with a population in excess of 71 million. It is also the most prosperous province in China, mainly due to its close links with and proximity to Hong Kong.

The wealth of Guangdong is mainly in Guangzhou and the other SEZs (Special Economic Zones) of Shenzhen, Zhuhai and Shatou, as well as the less well known cities in the Pearl River Delta – Dongguan, Panyu, ZhongShan and Shunde.

Dongguan is in fact now a large and growing city, attracting many of the world's well known names as investors into its conurbation.

Zhuhai

Another, perhaps not quite so well known, city attracting investment, is Zhuhai, situated in the south of Guangdong province, and possibly one of China's best kept secrets!

Zhuhai borders Macao to the south and Hong Kong is to the east, across the sea. It claims to be one of China's most popular tourist destinations and has the second largest international border crossing in China, with more than 100,000 passing through daily.

5

A recent publication cited six reasons for doing business in Zhuhai:

● Zhuhai has more than 20 years' experience of foreign investment and offers a range of preferential policies.

● The development and expansion of the Pearl River Delta will benefit the economies of Hong Kong and Macao, and also contribute to another quantum leap for the economy of Zhuhai.

● Zhuhai has the only deep water port in the western section of the Pearl River Delta and, as such, has the potential for developing into a significant, regional economic centre.

● The municipal government guarantees an efficient and fully supportive service for foreign investments.

● The region boasts a well educated workforce. There are more than 10 universities providing a continuous supply of skilled and qualified labour.

● Zhuhai is recognised as being a beautiful and clean coastal city, and has many awards for its environmental excellence. It claims to be one of the best working and living environments in China.

Focus on Zhuhai
The industries of foreign investment focus are:

● Electronics and information communications.

● Computer software development

● Biotech, pharmaceutical and medical equipment.

● Electrical equipment.

● Petrochemicals.

Zhuhai is famous for the biennial international aerospace and aviation exhibition which attracts business visitors, and tourists, from all over the world. Another major attraction is motor racing on Zhuhai's Formula One Race Track. Some of the best known world-class drivers attend this event, but they are probably outdone by the bus drivers from Hong Kong!

5

Financing Exports

Getting paid is an obvious necessity in any business so remember the saying 'an order is not an order until the money is in the bank'.

A Well Known Story

One 'scam' that occurs on a fairly regular basis in some parts of the world, is for an overseas client to start trading, on relatively small value terms and paying by L/C. The orders continue, increase in value, payments arrive on time and all is well. Then comes the 'sting'! Having established an element of trust, the buyer places a significantly larger value order and asks for open credit terms, and, yes, you've guessed, the goods are shipped based on trust and a reasonable track record, and the payment is never honoured. The 'con' is complete and the buyer moves on, leaving the supplier with a debt he will find difficult, if not impossible, to collect!

5

Case History

As an example, in 1997, when the Asian financial crisis occurred, we had a debt of about £70,000 outstanding in Indonesia. Our long term clients admitted straight away they could not pay this debt as the Rupiah had crashed against Sterling and the exchange rate had gone from about 6000 Rupiah to 20,000 Rupiah to £1.00, literally overnight! Payment of this debt, at that prohibitive rate of exchange, would have wiped out the company in Indonesia. We were able to claim against our Short Term Policy and within about 6 weeks, received 90 per cent of the debt against the policy. The company in Indonesia had agreed to make stage payments to us over 2 years and each time we received a transfer, we retained 10 per cent, and the balance was paid back to the insurer. We did eventually receive the funds in full, as did the insurer, within the two year period. Had we not had that cover, it could have been a serious loss for our company.

Short Term Finance

If you are a manufacturer or supplier of goods, securing the best payment terms to suit your own circumstances is important. Negotiating the first order is often cause for celebration and elation at the prospect of securing business in a competitive market, which could guarantee the medium-term future of your company. But receiving the first payment is all-important to your confidence of your customer.

Banks and other export advisors will recommend that payment should be by Confirmed International Letter of Credit (CILC) and, if you are UK-based, established with a London bank. The period of payment can be either 'at sight', which means you are paid within a couple of weeks of presenting the documents to the bank, or 30 days, 60 days, 90 days up to 180 days, usually from the date of the Bill of Lading. A CILC means that the confirming bank will pay you, providing all the documents are in order, irrespective of any problems in the originating country.

A Letter of Credit (L/C), without the bank's confirmation, is a normal way of obtaining payment and you will find it is quite usual to work on this basis, providing of course there are no political or underlying problems, either with the country or the client. The payment to your account will be transferred once the client has accepted the documents and agreed on the settlement with the originating bank.

If you are offering extended terms for payment against a CILC, then this may be discounted through the bank and you will receive the funds before the maturity term of the CILC. The banks make a charge for this facility and you have to consider whether the costs are worthwhile, compared to the interest charges incurred in funding the payment term. This can, however, be beneficial to your cash flow.

Another payment method is Cash Against Documents (CAD). This, in simple terms, means you are trusting your client and giving him open credit to pay you, on trust. You can send the documents through your bank for payment against Bills of Exchange, by which the bank keeps control of the documents until the client agrees to settle, as without the documents the client is

5

unable to clear the goods on arrival at the port of destination.

It is always wise to take professional advice from banks, Chambers of Commerce, Institutes of Export, etc, regarding the sensitive subject of getting paid, as there are many pitfalls.

Insurance against non-payment is available through Short Term policies available from NCM Direct [www.ncm-direct.com] and EulerTrade Indemnity Co Ltd [www.eulergroup.com] but, like all insurance companies, there are costs and conditions attached to receiving cover. An important factor of having Short Term Cover is to reveal this to your client.

Some customers, when they are aware you have an insurance against non-payment, will see it as an excuse for not paying you, knowing that you are covered.

Medium and Long Term Finance
If you are planning to invest in China then longer terms of finance will be needed.

There are three major sources of medium to long term finance offering the potential for preferential interest rates in a variety of currencies.

Multilateral Aid
The World Bank and the Asian Development Bank are the sources for these funds. The advantages are that little or no interest is payable and the term can be very long, more than 20 years. The disadvantages are that the Chinese Ministry of Finance will only use this assistance for top priority projects and the approval process can be extremely lengthy.

Major international banks with a presence in the region

China

Bank of China ; Standard Chartered Bank; HSBC; CITC Industrial Bank; China Merchants Bank; Industrial and Commercial Bank of China.

Hong Kong

HSBC; Standard Chartered Bank; Bank of China; First National City Bank; Shanghai Commercial Bank; Bank of America; Bank of East Asia.

Bilateral Aid

Funds are channelled through a UK Bank and a Chinese Bank. The financial advantages are you can have fixed interest rate finance and a choice of currency. The supplier can rest assured that payments will be honoured, usually on a 30-day term from receipt of documents in China. There are disadvantages in that the aid is tied and there are strict conditions concerning the actual type of project for which the aid is intended, ie, environmental, economic, etc. There can also be a protracted time in concluding the project approvals process.

Export Credit

Medium and long term export credit cover is available from Export Credits Guarantee Department (ECGD) to support the sale of capital goods and export projects in China. (see Chapter 2)

At one time, before privatisation, ECGD offered short term cover for exports but this is no longer available.

Import Restrictions

The legislation in China covering imports and exports is changing regularly and exporters are advised to contact their shipping agents for up-to-date information.

Most trading is conducted through state trading organisations and import licences are automatically granted when an order is placed.

Generally speaking, Hong Kong is a free port with very few trade restrictions. These restrictions relate to the import of rice, frozen or chilled meat, frozen poultry, and some other products, ranging from radioactive materials to pharmaceuticals and firearms.

Further information is available from Croner's *Reference Book for Exporters*, [www.croners.co.uk]

Exchange Controls

In China, the issue of a Letter of Credit guarantees availability of exchange.

There are no exchange controls in Hong Kong.

Taxation

For China, it is best to consult a financial expert or Trade Partners UK on the taxation system as very little is

5

made of this in economic reports and therefore it is important to understand what your liabilities will be before venturing into any investment arrangement.

Since joining the WTO, there have been some taxation changes but the actual tax system in China can differ according to the scope of your enterprise. A useful website is: [www.pwcglobal.com].

In Hong Kong, the tax system for foreign investors and businessmen is clearly defined.

• Low rate of tax on profits.

• Only income and profits derived from Hong Kong are subject to tax.

• No tax on capital gain, dividends or interest.

• Generous capital allowance.

• Low personal tax.

• The current profits tax rate is 16 per cent for corporations and 15 per cent for non-corporate taxpayers.

A useful website for taxation information in Hong Kong is: [www.info.gov.hk]

Shipping Arrangements

Seafreight

The most common form of transport is the "container", either 20ft (6m) or 40ft (12m) and more than 18 million of these were shipped into and out of Hong Kong in 2000. There are different types of container, ranging from the standard "dry" unit, refrigerated ("reefers") units, open topped, open sided and flat racks for transporting out of gauge equipment. The 'payloads' can vary from 22 tonnes to 28 tonnes and it is important to consider the weight-to-volume ratio of the goods being shipped. Experienced shipping, or freight agents, will assist and offer advice based on your own, specific requirements. You must also declare any hazardous or dangerous goods; special documentation is required and the containers must be labeled with the appropriate hazard information, before they can be shipped.

Airfreight

From the UK, Air China and British Airways World Cargo are just two of the many carriers offering services to both Hong Kong and Chinese destinations.

Airfreight is a more expensive but obviously faster method of getting your goods to the market, and for lighter cargoes, it is often the most expedient. The volume of air cargo traffic handled through Hong Kong International Airport is increasing and in 2000, more than 2.24 millions tonnes were dealt with.

In China, there are currently 142 airports and in cargo terms almost 4 million tonnes was handled, 201 tonnes being for the domestic market and the remainder for international destinations.

There is a multitude of shipping/freight agents dealing with both sea and airfreight and some recommendations feature later in this book.

Import Duties

As a consequence of opening its borders, China is gradually relaxing the duties paid on imports and the duty on many items has been reduced. Goods imported by the State trading organisations are free of duty.

Hong Kong is a duty free port. The only tariffs on imports apply to excise duty on alcoholic drinks and other alcoholic products, tobacco and hydrocarbon oil. The duties can be excessive, with 100 per cent on alcohol and hydrocarbon products and 60 per cent on wine.

These duties are reflected in the prices at the bar and also at the petrol pump.

Further information about duties is available from the China Unit, Trade Partners UK,

❏ Tel: +44 20 7215 4829 / 4830 or [www.tradepartners.gov.uk]

Intellectual Property & Trade Marks

The protection of Intellectual Property (IP) and Trade Marks is a major concern for any company investing in China. The principles behind Trade Mark legislation are basically the same in many countries but the formalities and protection afforded will vary from country to country.

5

It is reported that foreign firms who have not already sought protection for their marks or IP in specific countries will find they have actually been beaten to it by overseas or domestic competitors, and that similar or identical marks have already been registered. The major issue, and resultant litigation, over domain names serves to prove the point and how important it is to get in early.

Some advice recently given is as follows:

- Be aware of the risks.

- Identify your 'know how'.

- Read the regulations.

- Register your domain name (dot com.cn)

- Be aware of your potential partner.

- Maintain control. Be careful of contributing your Intellectual Property.

- Consult a lawyer specialising in Intellectual Property matters.

- If it goes wrong, seek professional advice and do as much homework as you can before making any commitments.

The government of Hong Kong SAR has its own Intellectual Property Department and comprehensive information can be found on website: [www.info.gov.hk/ipd]

China is a member of the International Convention for the Protection of Industrial Property.

The World Intellectual Property Organisation (WIPO) is based in Geneva and they publish a monthly journal, **Industrial Property**, containing translations of any new laws or orders affecting Trade Marks in a member country.

China Rising

An 'informed' forecast for the real GDP growth for China and its neighbouring countries in 2003 makes interesting reading:

China	7.7 per cent
Singapore	5.8 per cent

Malaysia   5.7 per cent

Thailand   4.2 per cent

Indonesia   4.2 per cent

The rise in domestic consumption is obviously a significant factor in the growth of the GDP, but it is well reported that China has its weaknesses as well – the main one being the financial sector, with a technically bankrupt banking system and a desperately low level of profitability from its domestic companies.

There is an obvious need for greater efficiency amongst established manufacturers and also a desire to acquire new technology, from the lowest level of industry to the high tech, sophisticated products and that is one reason why China has to open its doors even wider. These reforms will not happen overnight, but you can't change thousands of years of ideology and culture just by introducing new laws at the swipe of a pen, or bamboo paint brush. As has been said, many times, investing in China is a long haul, and don't expect results overnight.

In 2002, Daimler Chrysler, the US-German vehicle group, announced they were planning to invest around US$226 million over the next few years. This is in joint venture with Beijing Automotive Industry and the investment will finance the production of a series of new models. This commitment has been brought about by China's accession to the WTO in 2001.

A newspaper headline declared 'China exports first cars to US'. This news was reported in a major financial broad sheet in 2002 and related to 252 cars, manufactured by the Tianjin Auto Group, being sent on a trial basis to the USA, as they need to be tested to ensure they conform to American safety and emission standards.

The report indicated a potential volume of 25,000 cars could be exported over a five-year period, subject to the approvals being given.

Once again, 'the longest journey starts with a single step.'

China is the world's largest producer of cement but the demand outstrips production, according to the Institute

5

Cement

of Technical Information for Building Materials Industry in Beijing.

Every conceivable construction project needs cement. Cement is traded as a commodity item, and unofficial cartels have been known to exist in some countries, controlling the price of the "grey stuff". According to figures released by the State Statistics Bureau, China produced 275 million tonnes of cement in the first 6 months of 2000. This was an increase of more than 10 per cent on the same period in 1999.

Therefore, it goes without saying, that construction, and all its related industries, is doing well in China and you only have to witness the "forests" of tower cranes on the horizon of any city to fully appreciate the scope of development.

Glass, however, is a different matter. There are more than 50 float glass production lines in China and most of these are Chinese companies.

A joint venture company in Shanghai, Yaohua Pilkington, imported technology from the UK and the US company, PPG, have established a joint venture in Shenzhen.

Despite strict controls over the volume of production, there is currently an excess supply of sheet glass on the market and further controls have been implemented restricting any further expansion of this particular industry.

In a country the size and scope of China, getting the demand right must be an extremely fine art and, for that reason, much homework needs to be done before embarking upon any venture. That will obviously apply to any business and this is why taking expert advice is so important.

And Finally

If located in the UK, do not forget about our old friend, VAT!

VAT

The Customs and Excise department in the UK maintain extreme vigilance over export issues, particularly when it comes to avoidance of payment of VAT. If you export goods yourself, you do not need to charge VAT at the going rate, but you will need to keep scrupulous records of your transactions and shipments. Certificates of Shipment are a particularly important document as are

Bills of Lading and these are proof of shipment and export.

For exporters, the Customs & Excise rules are clearly defined and the old adage, "ignorance is no excuse" could not be more appropriate when it comes to duties payable!

A useful source of information on this subject is: [www.croners.co.uk]

Lucky Numbers

According to the order of Feng Shui, lucky numbers bring prosperity and the most open way of displaying this is through the number plates of cars. The lucky numbers are 1,6,7,8 & 9 with 8, pronounced 'phat' (prosperous growth or rich), being the most popular. The number 9 is the premier number and signifies fullness of heaven and earth.

The number 4 is considered to be extremely unpopular, and the "death" number, as it sounds like 'die' when translated into Chinese.

The Ministry of Public Security in China began issuing six digit licence plates during mid 2002, due to a rapid increase in vehicles over the last 10 years or so, and according to recent estimates, there are now more than 74 million vehicles registered in China.

Under these reforms, certain "lucky" licence plates will become invalid. They include plates with triple numbers, such as 888 and a police spokesman has been quoted as saying that these plates actually created superstition to a certain degree.

The new system for licence plates in China also bans those containing the same letter three times, although owners will be able to choose special combinations of letters and numbers under rules set by the police authority.

5

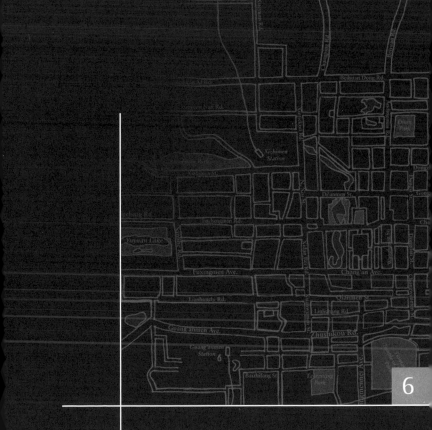

6

major industries

major industries

6

An overview of each of the
major industries of the nation
and where they stand today.

Major Industries

'Made in China'

It is almost impossible to pick up a newspaper or business magazine without reading or scanning an article about a well known or less known company name setting up a business venture or expanding existing operations in China.

Trade with China has been going on for centuries but China now features very strongly as a significant base for foreign companies in world market terms.

You only have to do your own simple market research by checking the origin of goods in stores in your own locality to begin to understand the importance China has as a manufacturing centre, and there will be quite a few surprises when it comes to famous brand names.

I recently bought a set of new golf clubs with an extremely well known brand name but a small label on the shaft declares "Made in China". I saw some very attractive dining room furniture in a multi-national store, also "Made in China". Those are but two examples of how China is beginning to influence the world in its ability to produce quality products.

China should not be just seen, as once it was, as a cheap country, and the old accolade, "Made in China", as a manufacturer of poor quality products. China has progressed far beyond those days and is now an extremely important force to be reckoned with and respected, in world market terms.

You just have to consider the well known brand names that now have a presence in China to fully appreciate how far China has come over the last two decades. Where they are now is just like the tip of the iceberg when it comes to what they have to offer for the future.

The only problem about relying upon one, vastly emerging nation, is the "eggs in one basket" syndrome! If China becomes such an important, and powerful nation of manufacturers, can it hold the rest of the world to ransom over the supply and prices of the goods on offer? Conversely, if the rest of the world refuses to buy, then China will not have a market. An interesting conundrum and one, that hopefully we will not have to confront in our own lifetime!

6

Much has been written in recent times about the burgeoning domestic market in China and, with a population of 1.3 billion people, the rise, in economic terms, of the middle classes is an effective indicator for significant progress in the demands of the populace. As people acquire wealth, they demand, and expect, a better standard of living for themselves and also for their offspring.

However, the greatest attraction for a country's government is in its ability to generate foreign exchange, and this is produced by exporting manufactured goods, services and also from invisible earnings.

For China to expand its base it has to attract Foreign Direct Investment (FDI) and, whilst no absolute figures are available, it is reported that in the first 6 months of 2001, contracted FDI was nearly US$34 billion, and this was an increase of 38% on the first half of 2000.

6

Bikes

As the automobile industries grow and the demand for cars increases in China, the need for the traditional form of transport, the bicycle, diminishes. One of the world's largest bicycle manufacturers, the Shenzhen Bicycle Company, has seen its fortunes decrease over the last 5 years, resulting in considerable financial losses over the same period.

Chinese Exports

The Chinese government has a policy of extending non-state companies' rights to encourage export growth, and in 2001, they were proactive by raising tax rebates for export. An example of this was on the rebate for cloth and yarn, which was increased from 15 per cent to 17 per cent.

The following figures indicate the value and percentage of increase of Chinese exports for main commodities.:

Commodity	(US $ billions)	% change
Hi-tech products	20.60	31.40
Garments & accessories	16.20	1.60
Textiles (Raw materials & finished goods)	8.40	6.00
Footwear	5.00	2.20
Plastic products	2.40	1.50
Toys	2.00	13.80
Furniture	2.00	8.40
Aquatic products	1.20	12.90
Refined oil	1.10	11.80
Rolled steel	0.90	16.70
Crude oil	0.80	34.00

Foreign Investment

Since China's accession to the WTO in 2001, and the changes in many laws and rules being brought about, China has become even more attractive to foreign investors.

In the early months of 2002, foreign banks and insurance companies in China were given licences to undertake foreign currency transactions with Chinese customers.

A number of leading insurance companies have set up JVs with mainland partners and are able to offer insurance services to indigenous Chinese customers. (The man from the "PRU" eventually arrives in China!)

Having already established a presence in China, these financial institutions were at last able to benefit from China's new foreign investment regime, thanks to its accord with the WTO in late 2001.

Another advantage to benefit FDI's is the opening up of previously closed or highly restricted business sectors and these include:

- Banking

- Securities

6

- Telecommunications

- Trading

- Distribution

- Tourism

In a further relaxation of rules still yet to come, foreign firms will be able to set up WFOEs (Wholly Foreign Owned Enterprises) in businesses such as: advertising, real estate and management consulting

However, for some strategic sectors, the old arrangement of majority Chinese ownership remains in place.

Confused? The relaxation of the laws and rules, dates of when effective, what type of business structure should you consider, where is the best location to set up your business, are all very good questions and that is why, sound, professional advice is critical to your decision to be in China.

The protocol on China's accession to the WTO and some related documents can be viewed, in English, on the MOFTEC website: www.moftec.gov.cn/moftec_cn/wto/wtolaw.html

As an example of how companies are finding their way through the maze of rules and regulations, official figures issued by MOFTEC for 2001 show that paid up foreign investments reached a record level of US$46.8 billion, which was an increase of nearly 15 per cent on 2000. The contracted FDI figure for the same period was US$69 billion, showing an increase of 10.4 per cent.

Local Manufacture

The main, underlying reasons for any company, manufacturing or otherwise, to establish a business relationship in China are lower production costs, increased margins and also greater volume of activity.

Also, access to the Chinese domestic market is an important factor plus having the advantage of being close to emerging markets in the region.

This is very obvious from the volume of shipping containers to be located in Chinese ports and also Hong Kong. For this very reason, the freight rates on offer for shipments from European ports to China and Hong Kong are currently very low in relation to the actual cost. The shipping lines need the empty containers in China and Hong Kong to cope with the volume of demand for shipments to Europe and the USA. This is where the lines make up the difference in freight costs by having different, more expensive, tariffs for the return journey. It is based on the supply and demand principle.

China may not necessarily have the cheapest manufacturing unit costs in South East Asia or the Far East, but it is capable of producing volume at what is often described as a "cost effective" price. Quality has improved and also China has the advantage of being politically stable.

It has a rapidly increasing infrastructure, capable of coping with the very exacting demands of foreign companies investing in China, and whilst these resources may at times seem strained, or deficient in some respects, the Chinese government is putting much emphasis on improving and acceding to the wishes of foreign investors.

Olympic Games 2008

In 2008, Beijing will host the 29th Olympic Games and as a result, it is predicted that the Chinese capital will undergo the biggest, single construction boom in its 3000 year history. The process of preparing for the Olympic Games will be a significant boost for the economy and the affects will be felt right throughout China.

With the motto "New Beijing, Great Olympics", and an aim to host a "Green Olympics", a "Hi-tech Olympics" and the "People's Olympics", Beijing is preparing itself to become a truly international city.

The budget proposals amount to expenditure of about US$22 billion, and this will be spent on municipal infrastructure and sports venues. Half of the investment will be allocated to developing the transportation infrastructure, tripling the length of the city's roads and quadrupling the capacity of the underground (metro) system.

From this budget, US$40 million has been allocated to upgrade the healthcare facilities and there are plans to spend US$400 million on upgrading the communications and technology infrastructure.

6

Beijing already has 13 sports venues which will be renovated and upgraded, and a further 19 sports venues will be constructed specifically for the Olympic Games.

It is reported that Chinese and foreign investors will have equal opportunities to win contracts for projects through an open bidding system, but as in many cases, having a local presence will be a significant factor. The rules for the open bidding scheme can be obtained by contacting the Beijing Olympic Games Organising Committee (BOGOC) whose website is: [www.beijing-2008.org.cn]

Major Opportunities

The process of preparing for such a massive event involves virtually every conceivable aspect of industry, from:

Architects, consultants, interior designers, landscape architects, transportation specialists

To suppliers of:

Building Materials, heating and ventilation, telecom systems, temporary housing, stadia seating, internet (broadband) systems, electronic systems, catering facilities and food, beds and ancillary items, water treatment

The list of essential items and services for such a project is endless and the opportunities immense.

Benefits

Hosting the games will be of major importance to the Chinese government and there are unanswered questions as to where the vast sum of US$22 billion will come from, but it is reported that the Beijing Government will contribute a small proportion, and the remaining costs are expected to emanate from central government and Chinese and foreign investors.

One important source of revenue, American prime time television advertising, is likely to be limited because of the 12 hour time difference between Beijing and the USA. This, in previous games, has been a major source of revenue for the International Olympic Committee (IOC) and obviously needs to be filled if the financial commitments are to be realised.

Private citizens are expected to be asked to contribute as are employees of state owned enterprises and the government hopes to raise at least US$180 million through state run lotteries.

Hong Kong's Challenge

Hong Kong, with its border with China to the north and natural boundaries of the sea in other directions, has a major difficulty in coping with the disposal of waste.

During the 1990s, Hong Kong developed three massive landfill sites, with a total capacity of about 135 million cubic metres and with inputs to these landfills currently at 16,000 tonnes per day, it is expected that these sites will be full by 2012.

The Hong Kong Government is aware of the problem and a report *Environment 2002* clearly states that solutions need to be found by 2004 at the latest to avoid seeing waste piling up on the streets.

The issue is likely to be a test of the Hong Kong Government's resolve on the environment and also there will be excellent long term business opportunities for companies involved in the waste management industries.'

The Race is On

Although 2008 seems a way off from the present time, many foreign companies have already made their mark and many more will have an equal chance to bid for infrastructure projects related to the games.

General Motors (GM) have concluded an exclusive car sponsorship with the Olympic Committee for 4 years and the Canadian company, SNC-Lavalin Group, are reported to have secured the contract to assist with construction of new underground (metro) railway lines, valued at about US$1.5 billion.

Although a majority of the games events will be held in and around Beijing, China as a whole will benefit and five other cities will host specific competitions:

Watersport events will take place in the port and holiday resort city of Qingdao. Football (soccer) matches will be played in Tianjin, Shanghai, Qinhuangdao and Shenyang, a major industrial city north of Beijing.

The logistics of moving competitors around, accommodating teams and all their followers is a significant task and one that will require a well oiled and efficient infrastructure.

6

In Beijing itself, the Olympic Village will have a land area of 80 hectares and a total building floor area of 470,000 square meters. It will be designed to accommodate 17,600 athletes and team officials.

After the games, the Paralympics will take place, and this will also create substantial business opportunities for companies involved in supporting the multi-various needs of the disabled athletes.

Once the whole 29th Olympic Games are over, the Village will become a residential area for the inhabitants of Beijing.

A spokesman for the National Bureau of Statistics has been quoted as saying "The success of the Olympic bid will create a more stable society, provide opportunities to develop our economy and open China up further to the outside world."

Manufacturing

It is predicted that by 2006, China might well have replaced Germany as the world's third largest manufacturing country. In 2000, the league was headed by USA, Japan and Germany with China in fourth place but is estimated that Chinese industrial output will grow by 10 per cent annually from 2002 – 2006, placing China third in the world table.

Medicine and Health Care

Figures released in 2002 put the number of people infected with the HIV virus well in excess of 1 million compared to lower "official figures" previously announced.

Tuberculosis (TB) is the leading infectious cause of death in China and the World Bank has financed a programme to control infectious and endemic diseases.

In addition to an extension of financing by the World Bank, the UK Department for International Development has also given China a grant to enable money to be lent to provinces at concessional rates.

The demand for medicines and antibiotics will inevitably increase and the world's best known pharmaceutical firms are already well in evidence in China.

It is perhaps a strange fact, but as nations become more prosperous, the average weight per person seems to increase and China now has a US$1 billion market in 'weight loss' products. These include slimming soups, herbal remedies and laxatives.

By 2006, Shanghai should have built up to five new hospitals and improved its healthcare facilities. City officials are also encouraging the development of more private hospitals and clinics in the suburbs to cope with the shift in population away from the city centre. No doubt, similar schemes will follow in other cities.

Healthcare in China is effectively governed by four separate ministry level organisations:

• The Ministry of Health – responsible for the management of healthcare institutions and training of personnel.

• The State Drug Administration (SDA) – regulates the use and production of medical devices and pharmaceutical products.

• The State Administration for Traditional Chinese Medicines.

• The Ministry of Labour and Social Security – responsible for welfare and the establishment of a medical insurance system.

Oil & Gas

Crude oil and refined oil feature in China's exports and much activity is centered around the South China Sea and also more recently, the Yellow Sea.

The state-owned China National Offshore Oil Company (CNOOC) and their subsidiary China Offshore Nanhai West Corporation have awarded contracts in the Panyu Field where a "floating, production, storage and offloading" (FPSO) facility is being constructed. The first oil is scheduled for the end of 2003.

In the Daqing region of north east China, China National Petroleum (PetroChina) has plans to invest US$700 million in the Sino-Russian pipeline with a Russian financial commitment approaching US$ 1 billion. The proposed 2,400 km pipeline will supply Siberian crude oil to refineries in Daqing and is expected to be on stream by 2005.

6

There is an increasing reliance on expensive, imported crude oil, so the need to become more self sufficient with locally produced oil is obviously a major concern for the Chinese government. As private cars become more affordable, the consumption of oil is expected to increase by 80 per cent by 2010.

China has rich reserves of natural gas and in Beijing alone, there are more than 20,000 buses, most of which run on natural gas and the intention is to convert all public transport to this form of propellant, with other cities following suit.

In 2001, it was reported that Chinese geologists had found evidence of oil reserves in the southern part of the Yellow Sea and estimate there may be anything from 2 billion to nearly 3 billion tonnes of oil and gas under the seabed.

Coal

This continues to be a prominent industry in China, but usually for the wrong reasons as safety in coal mines is a major issue and one of great cause for concern.

6

China is investing more in the development of coal technology and coal liquefying technology was one of the 12 priority items listed in the last five-year plan of the State Development Planning Commission.

Logistics

The 'logistics' industry incorporates many of the services of getting mail, packages, goods, etc, from A to B, at the most efficient and cost effective rates. Competition in this industry is strong but there are many good opportunities available in a country the size of China.

Postal services, courier deliveries, airfreight, seafreight, container storage, bonded warehouses, distribution of goods are all constituents of logistics available to many sectors of industry.

Automobiles

The list of major motor manufacturers already investing in China is endless and all the "household" names are well established in what is rapidly becoming a competitive market, especially in the luxury bracket.

In Beijing, the number of motor vehicles is rapidly approaching 2 million with about 1 million being privately owned. During the period January – March 2002, it was reported that more than 500,000 motor vehicles were registered and this was an increase of about one third on the same period for 2001.

Optoelectronics
This is considered to be one of the major growth industries in China, particularly for use within consumer goods such as digital cameras, LCD television sets and other appropriate electronic items.

The industry has shown a considerable expansion factor, particularly in the regions of Changchun, Wuhan and Guangzhou.

Food and Drink
Although China produces some of the most delicious and interesting foods imaginable, the tastes of the indigenous population are rapidly changing and McDonalds are well in evidence wherever you travel, although they have been instructed to remove their distinctive signs as they were considered to "visually pollute" the environment.

KFC and Pizza Hut, which are both owned by Tricon Global Restaurants Inc, are also making their mark on the landscape.

Chocolate is also very much a delicacy for the Chinese and street billboards advertise the products available. The market is very small by Western standards, but it is one that seems to be gathering momentum as time passes.

Since China's accession to WTO in 2001, it is predicted that the period up to about 2006 will be critical to the development of food and drink distribution.

Christmas Bonus
It may seem strange to think of Christmas in terms of China but Shenzhen is reputedly the world's largest Christmas products exporter in the world, and I always thought Father Christmas came from the North Pole!

Shenzhen also grows and sells more than US$100 million worth of Christmas trees to the USA each year.

6

Environment

China's Challenge

The use of natural gas to power buses and taxis is well established within major cities in China and this will help to overcome the pollution problems that sometimes occur on the streets.

Water is to be diverted via a canal from the Yangtze River in the south to drought stricken areas in the north of China. The Ministry of Water Resources has literally been "swamped" by overseas companies enquiring about the project, which should start sometime in 2002.

The same ministry also has plans to provide 60 per cent of inhabitants in cities of more than 500,000 with sewerage disposal facilities and the aim is to complete this programme by 2005. (On that basis, 40 per cent of the cities population will not have facilities for sewerage disposal!)

6

Shenzhen, PRC

In 1981, Shenzhen became a Special Economic Zone and many Hong Kong companies set up factory units there, attracted by the competitive rates, cheap labour and proximity to Hong Kong.

Shenzhen, in Guangdong province, is now one of China's most prosperous cities.

The deserts in the northern provinces of China are attracting the attention of the Chinese government as the deserts are encroaching on arable land because of over use and lack of water resources. Hence the need for the water canal from the Yellow River.

The government is said to be working on laws to forbid eco-destructive activities in the desert areas and to encourage and attract foreign investment to help with the replanting of these wastelands.

Hong Kong's Challenge

Construction

This is a major industrial sector for China and finding your way around all the various Chinese government ministries can be a nightmare.

The Three Gorges Dam Project has had a high profile for a long time and the investment needed is huge, by any standards.

As mentioned earlier, the Olympic Games in 2008 is attracting a massive amount of attention. The budget for this whole project is colossal and is already attracting attention from companies worldwide.

There is a growing priority being given to environmental projects, bridges, transportation systems, expansion of airports, pipelines, ports, highways, etc. In fact, the list goes on and on!

Many UK, European, American and Australian companies are well established in China and these include architects, consultants, engineers, construction companies, quantity surveyors and all disciplines connected with the construction industry.

In this respect, Hong Kong has a significant stake in construction activities, particularly in Southern China, where Hong Kong developers have been active for many years.

Building Materials
Obviously, for any construction project, no matter the location, the supply of building materials is an essential need.

The Chinese construction market has become far more open, international and mature in its expectations and the increase in disposable income is having a positive affect on the quality of products used on all aspects of the project, particularly condominiums where style and finish are important to the buyer.

A major market for good quality, and the latest fashion, styles, colours, etc, of decorating materials is also being driven by the demands of a more sophisticated Chinese consumer. It is a recognised fact that, in China, the use of building materials continues to grow at a faster rate than the overall economic growth of the country.

Do-It-Yourself
The DIY, or more likely, the "do it for me" market in China is expanding fast and the British company, B&Q, had, by 2002, established itself well on the market in Shanghai and by 2006 aims to have at least 50 stores throughout China.

6

In 1999, B&Q became the first merchandising joint venture in the building materials industry in China and it seems the prospects for future growth in this sector are considerable. B&Q are selling predominantly locally sourced products with some imported products that cannot be found in China. The British company are the third largest DIY company in China following close behind domestic operators Home Mart, who have five stores and No 9 with three stores.

The DIY market is growing fast in China and is a major contributor to consumer spending.

Fashion

Since the mid 1990s, the change in the Chinese fashion industry has been dramatic and there is now a complete industry featuring design, manufacturing and finishing plus all the spin off business of advertising and fashion publicity, including trendy, glossy magazines.

In the earlier part of the last decade, China did not have a single design college and fashion, as such, lacked any sophistication. Clothes were purely functional items and any item considered "fashionable" was usually copied from western styles or imported by friends or relatives who had the opportunity of travelling overseas.

It is said by the Chinese that British companies have been slow in responding to the business opportunities fashion offers in China, but there have been some examples of success, particularly in the more creative designs and ideas. Burberry, Aquascutum, DAKS and London Fog are ones that come to mind.

Some very well known French, Italian and US labels have succeeded in China but there is a vast, potential market waiting for companies to make the appropriate effort.

The rewards are there and you only have to see the extent of the fashion industry in Hong Kong to fully appreciate the scale of the industry. In fact, it is generally known that many garments labelled "Made in Hong Kong" were actually made in the Guangzhou/Shenzhen region.

China has two main national fashion shows each year, one in Dalian and the other in Beijing. Qingdao is also trying hard to muscle in on the act by organising its own international fashion week. The China Fashion Week in

6

Beijing is dedicated to Chinese designers on a competitive basis. The Dalian Show is for manufacturers to display their wares and latest designs on a shop front basis, where the main visitors are wholesalers and retailers.

The need for good publicity, advertising and promotion is essential in any business but especially so in the fashion industry. Locally produced glossy magazines are plentiful and match those from the West in terms of content and style.

Education

This is another of the growth "industries" in China and Chinese students are particularly keen to learn English and study at English speaking colleges and universities outside China.

Executive MBAs are becoming very popular qualifications and it is estimated that there are more than 50,000 Chinese students in American universities each year.

The number of Chinese students in the UK is also significant and growing, as can be seen by the increasing number of multi-sector trade missions leaving UK shores on a regular basis. These trade missions frequently include representatives from business schools, colleges and universities, travelling to attract students for placements at their particular institutions.

6

On the upside, it is reported that in 2002 a record of 86 British universities and educational organisations attended a two day British Education Exhibition in Shanghai. The booths and stands of those displaying their wares were besieged by crowds of Chinese students eager to study at such well known seats of learning. This just goes to prove that the only real way of doing business in China is to be there!

The British Council, The British Embassy, TP UK and CBBC can all provide specific contacts, if required.

There is however a downside to this for China, as according to a China government report in 2002, of 380,000 Chinese people who travelled overseas to study since the open policy began in 1978, only 130,000 have returned.

6

During the Cultural Revolution education suffered a significant setback when schools closed and teachers and intellectuals were accorded the title 'the stinking ninth category'.

It is now recognised in China that education has a major role to play in the modernisation process and that education is a significant industry in itself, and one that is growing rapidly. Ironically, the government does not have sufficient resources to devote to education and the per capita expenditure is low. Schools, colleges and universities have had to resort to fundraising by organising workshops or factories or to selling their expertise to outside parties. With an ever increasing number of Chinese seeking education abroad in Europe, North America and Australia, only about one-third of these overseas students has returned to China and, after the mass demonstrations in Tiananmen Square in 1989, the government announced that graduates would be required to work in China for at least 5 years before undertaking any post-graduate studies overseas. In the meantime, the government has adopted preferential policies specifically to attract students back to China by creating job opportunities in Shenzhen and other Special Economic Zones.

Science and Technology
Since the 10th Five Year Plan was announced, three priority areas for development in these sectors were identified:

1. High Technology focusing on IT, biology, new materials, manufacturing, aerospace and aviation, ie, getting into the 21st century.

2. Upgrading the technological levels of traditional industries, ie, making them more efficient and profit driven.

3. Having a new science and technological system that is compatible with the requirements of a market economy, ie, making certain that new developments have a place in the market and producing what is needed.

With the accession to WTO, these priorities will have opened up new business opportunities for foreign investors in IT support services, consulting, financial services, human resources and many other, professional, related service industries.

Tourism

You cannot pick up a travel supplement from a newspaper without noticing the vast number of 'special deals' and 'offers' for holidays and tours to China and Hong Kong.

The choice is prodigious, the prices competitive and the sightseeing tours wondrous. They take in the Great Wall to the north of Beijing and the Forbidden City, The Summer Palace, Tiananmen Square and the Ming Tombs, all located in the environs of Beijing.

In the west you have the Terracotta Army at Xian, to the east is Shanghai with its famous Bund on the Huangpu River, and many other sights and delights in the southern province of Guangdong.

Tourism is a major industry and earner of foreign currency for China. First class hotels are springing up like mushrooms in the main tourist areas and major cities of China.

This also includes Hong Kong, where tourism is a very significant earner of foreign currency, with tourists passing through, either en route to China or to Australasia, as a "stop over" for a few days.

6

Other Industries

Private Sector

The private sector received much attention in the 10th Five Year Plan and private companies would be encouraged by the state to create "a fair competition environment for enterprises with different forms of ownership".

According to the Ministry of Labour, in the first quarter of 2002, China's private sector created nearly a third of all new job opportunities in the country. Private firms also produce about one third of China's entire GDP.

Anti-Dumping

Being a relatively low cost producing nation, China is very much aware of the effects and implications of having products 'dumped' on its own doorstep by other Far East countries with a lower cost base.

In January 2002, China's anti-dumping statute came into force and an "anti-dumping tax" can be imposed on any products imported into China at a price lower than the actual export value. The purpose of this law, and tax, is to protect domestic enterprises from damage to their own business, but policing such a venture is a huge task.

'Made in Hong Kong'

The growth of Hong Kong has been fuelled by trade, although many companies have moved their manufacturing bases to cheaper locations in China, particularly the Pearl River delta region.

The manufacturing sector is export orientated and although many of the items are made in China the cross-boundary traffic has shown a remarkable increase. You only have to travel through the border by car and experience the high volume of container traffic waiting to be checked by customs on both sides of the border, to fully appreciate the extent of flow of trade between the two partners.

Hong Kong does still retain many manufacturing units, especially in the New Territories, where space is less confined and also there is less traffic congestion. The manufacturing industry is dominated by SMEs (Small and Medium Sized Enterprises) and many of these firms are associated with much larger organisations outside Hong Kong.

Hong Kong is one of the world's largest exporters of clothing, toys, textiles, watches and costume jewellery, and in terms of employment, the clothing industry is the largest employer. This includes those employed in the wearing apparel and textiles industries.

The printing and publishing industry in Hong Kong is said to be the fourth largest in the world. Other significant employers in Hong Kong are:

- Machinery, equipment & parts

- Food, beverage & tobacco

Hong Kong is the most important source of external direct investment in China and most of this is concentrated in Guangdong province, around the Pearl River Delta.

Around 5 million Chinese workers in Guangdong province are working for Hong Kong companies, which

6

is 21 times the size of Hong Kong's own manufacturing workforce.

Hong Kong businessmen have extended their involvement in businesses in China by investing in real estate, condominium developments, hotels, restaurants, tourism, and infrastructure projects.

Reciprocally, China is probably the largest external investor in Hong Kong. This investment covers a wide range of business activities, including, imports/exports ; wholesale/retail; transportation; warehousing; banking; real estate; hotels; manufacturing and infrastructure.

Endless Opportunities

The opportunities for doing business in China and Hong Kong are infinite. If you think of an industry and then consider all the "spin off" prospects, or side industries servicing the main body, the list will be endless.

The Chinese are hungry for knowledge, they are in need of new technology, new products and new ideas. They have the desire, the space and the ability to improve their scope of activities, but they need the foreign investment and know-how to achieve these ends.

Environmental Challenge

Honk Kong, with its border with China to the north and natural boundaries of the sea in other directions, has a major difficulty in coping with the disposal of waste.

During the 1990s, Hong Kong developed three massive landfill sites, with a total capacity of about 135 million cubic metres and with inputs to these landfills currently at 16,000 tonnes per day, it is expected that these sites will be full by 2012.

The Hong Kong Government is aware of the problem and a report 'Environment 2002' clearly states that solutions need to be found by 2004 at the latest to avoid seeing waste piling up on the streets.

The issue is likely to be a test of the Hong Kong government's resolve on the environment and also there will be excellent opportunities for companies involved in the waste management industries.

6

Rice

As might be expected, with such a large landmass, China is the world's leading producer of rice.

China grows two crops of rice each year and produces about 180 million tonnes annually, of which, more than 10% of this total is exported. Traditional buyers of Chinese rice are Cuba, Iraq, Russia, North Korea and Libya.

A large, strategic stock of rice, estimated at 20 million tonnes, is believed to held by Beijing.

Ironically, Thailand is reputed to be the worlds' main rice exporter and China imports about 200,000 tonnes of rice, mostly the fragrant variety, from Thailand.

6

7

how to set up a
permanent operation

how to set up a permanent operation

The aim of this section is to provide a sweeping overview for the visitor who is considering the possibility of a local office. Here are some of the pitfalls and benefits, an insight into the legal situation, and some of the major issues to be considered, such as recruiting, finding premises, etc.

The purpose of this chapter is to provide a general overview of the pitfalls and advantages of establishing a permanent business operation in China.

Because of the rapidly changing situation in China and Hong Kong, it is impossible to be precise and accurate about all the circumstances. This section is intended purely as an insight into the process of generating business, where to locate, how to choose the right partner, who to turn to for help and information, the legal situation, etc.

A Long Haul

Factors to consider when contemplating setting up a business venture in China are:

Time – because it will not happen overnight and there will be many frustrations along the way;

Effort – as you will need to visit the market many times to get to know your potential partners and to really understand the business culture and the methods of doing business;

Determination – essential in being able to reach your goal without throwing in the towel along the way;

Financial capacity – because it is important to retain 'face' and be able to put your money where your mouth is when it comes to signing the MOU (Memorandum of Understanding) for your commitment for investing in the future in China.

And finally, a strong desire to succeed – maintain the momentum, to keep up the pressure on your new partner and to ensure the business continues along lines acceptable to you and your shareholders or financiers.

General Guidelines

Before attempting to set up a joint venture in China:

● Do your research thoroughly and establish that a market exists for whatever it is that you produce.

● Target the opportunities, meet potential customers and decide on a firm strategy for your sales.

● Are the firms you are talking to agents, distributors or end users? The answer will determine your pricing

A Long Haul

7

structure; do you really want to deal through middle men if your main customers are end users or OEMs (Original Equipment Manufacturers)? Understanding the characteristics of the various different markets is essential.

● Focus on what you want to achieve and try not to be diverted by vague promises of vast volume orders, multimillion deals, etc.

● Be aware there are companies that collect agencies to represent foreign companies and seem to have an endless list of company logos on their letterheads or literature. They are very active when you visit and spend time with their sales team but soon forget you when you leave.

So you have identified your business partner and agreed on terms for concluding the first order. Delivery details, payment terms are confirmed by both parties and you have a celebratory dinner and the customary drink or two.

Signing the first deal can be the catalyst to securing more business, and the beginning of your entry into a market that could change the fortunes of your company.

If, however, months – even years – pass without securing an order, it is time to question your approach to the market and sales philosophy. Was it the wrong market? Were you in the wrong location? Did you have poorly informed salesmen? Were the third party's mark-ups too high, or were your products not right for the market?

If you feel that your local contact, or their lack of enthusiasm, may be the reason why you have had a poor start on the market, then you will have lost only time, and not a great deal of money. You will also have gained some valuable experience along the way.

If you are determined to succeed, the time may not have been wasted, positive contacts appear from the most unlikely sources.

Local conformity
You must establish that your products conform with local regulations, of which there are many. Each province in China has its own Test Authority and many products need to be tested independently before they can enter the market place. Acceptance of your product in one

province is no guarantee that it will be accepted in another province. The chances are you will need to go through separate tests for each province, but then this is where the strength of your local partner, and his *guangxi* can come into force.

Establishing a Representative Office

Once you have secured orders and are comfortable with your local arrangement, then it is time to think seriously about setting up a representative office.

You may want to enlarge your operation and feel the first contact is not capable of undertaking such a venture in which case an alliance partner, who can help to defray costs by sharing facilities, may suit you better.

The China Britain Business Council (CBBC) offers its Launchpad Scheme to British companies and having a representative office in a suite of like-minded British companies can have many benefits and potential for spin-off business opportunities through the employment of competent local staff.

The management of these local staff will be a critical factor in the success or failure of your enterprise. Language and communications are obviously potential difficulties, but there is an increasing number of English-speaking Chinese graduates looking for positions with Western companies, so the problem is not insurmountable.

By having your own representative office, you can exercise greater control of your China operations, and be able to respond more rapidly to market conditions.

Expansion

As confidence in the representative office grows, and sales and profits materialise, expansion should be part of your strategy. Appointing distributors, sales agents, etc, in different provinces and increasing your outlets throughout China as part of a planned programme will be essential to the development of your business.

In the medium term, there are several options available to you and it may be worth considering establishing a Wholly Owned Foreign Enterprise (WOFE) to act as a

7

China holding company. It all depends on your budgetary plans and also the financial strength of your home base. There is no point in entering into arrangements for expansion in export markets if it is going to impact upon your domestic situation.

This set up may not provide the security of a formal Chinese Holding Company (CHC) but could be a more practical starting point for a small to medium sized enterprise (SME).

Another option is to work alongside an existing Foreign Investment Enterprise (FIE) who is in a complementary sector of industry, who has a mature country-wide sales and distribution network and is prepared for you to work alongside them, thus reducing their own overheads.

Manufacturing base

Once again, as part of the overall strategy for being in China, from the outset your long-term plans should include the eventual setting up of your own manufacturing base.

By being closely involved in the local business community and talking to other foreign investors and compatriots, you will be able to benefit from their experience, mistakes, and hopefully their advice as to whether you should opt for a JV or a WOFE.

Guidelines for Expansion

Investigate the market place thoroughly, check out the competition and assess the potential for investing in China on a long-term basis.

Consider the impact such a radical move will have on your own domestic business. Will you need to eventually close a factory or office to offset the opening of similar facilities in China?

Take your time, win orders and get yourself established as a brand or a name on the market before making any move towards investment.

If, as a FIE, you enter into a joint venture agreement, keep the manufacturing process and facilities separate from the sales and distribution set up. There are few, if any, successful Chinese manufacturers with effective combined sales and distribution arrangements. The cultures of manufacturing and sales should be kept apart and also accounted separately. Don't forget, China is a huge and diverse country and is not one market, but a cluster of markets.

For this reason, you should plan, in the long term, for regional manufacturing facilities and not necessarily with the same partner, whilst maintaining control of the sales and distribution network.

Look at new ideas for improving production methods, consider your sources of raw materials, and keep up to date with the competition in China.

Consider a limited assembly operation in a WOFE form, which would give you legal and direct control over your sales and distribution. But check, and double check, the customs duties on imported products even when used as components in products finally assembled in China under the Six Pillars of Industry Plan – industry plans to be able to produce 'Complete Sets of Equipment', i.e, no

---

Corruption

7

Corruption, particularly within State Organisations, is not unknown – the official advice is don't get involved. Corruption is a capital offence and recently there have, been a number of high profile court cases involving state officials and the ubiquitous brown envelopes. Corruption must not be confused with *guanxi*; the two are totally different.

Hong Kong has very strong anti-corruption laws and the Independent Commission Against Corruption, commonly known as the ICAC, fights corruption on three fronts, investigation, prevention and education. According to the ICAC, corruption is under control in Hong Kong. The ICAC certainly commands respect within the business community and a high degree of confidence amongst the general public. To help firms combat corruption, the ICAC has produced easy-to-use *Best Practice Packages* on ways to highlight, and minimise corruption opportunities in vulnerable sectors such as procurement, staff administration, information system security, contract letting and administration. A useful website for more information is: [www.info.gov.hk/info/icac.htm]

reliance upon imported goods or components, no matter how insignificant or technical. China in this bold move plans to be totally self-sufficient in industry.

Location

● Look at the prospects for exporting from China as there are tax incentives for bringing foreign currency into the country and exports are a major source of income.

● If you already have good business dealings with a company based in Hong Kong, then consider using them for your entry into China, and especially into the industrial areas between Shenzhen and Guangzhou, which includes the rapidly expanding city of Dong Guan.

● Avoid attempting to start in multiple locations. China is too big for that.

● Check with Trade Partners UK – China Unit, or CBBC for advice if you are uncertain about the right place to set up your business.

● Think about the logistics of distribution, not only for the domestic market but for export as well.

Distribution

Once you have set up your manufacturing plant, distributing your goods is of the essence. Distribution is a major part of the supply chain and, as in most business cultures around the world, a sophisticated element of the business environment. China presents a challenge, but the systems are changing as the needs increase.

In general, the quality of warehousing facilities in China is poor, with low grade mechanical handling equipment. Labour is plentiful – and cheap compared to a forklift truck. Damage to goods is not uncommon. Major foreign investors often establish their own, directly supervised, warehouses with security, or arrange supervision of third party warehouse facilities to overcome this problem.

There are a growing number of FIEs who have seen the gap in the market and are able to provide secure and reliable warehousing services together with a distribution network.

Goods can be moved by road, rail, air and water. The Chinese government has a vast budget to improve existing roads and build new highways, but road transport can be an expensive means of distribution. Airfreight is the most expensive form of transportation and will be used for the urgent delivery of smaller components or replacements for goods previously damaged in transit by other means. Water transport is widely used for bulky goods, but road transport will be needed to carry the goods from port to final destination. Rail, which is predominantly a State monopoly, provides the cheapest form of transport but has a reputation for being unreliable and relatively slow.

Hong Kong as Staging Post

As mentioned, dealing with a Hong Kong company for business into Southern China is a relatively easy way to get established. The disadvantage is that higher overheads in Hong Kong mean increased loss, and there is also the fact that you will not be in complete control of any dealings.

7

Communications

Hong Kong has one of the highest densities of telephones in the world, with about 73 telephones or 58 lines per 100 people.

It is also the first major city in the world to have a fully digitised telephone network system, which is local Fixed Telecommunications Network Service (FTNS). As of January 2002, there were 5.7 million subscribers of cellular telephone services and it is expected the high growth rate of the mobile phone will continue.

I will always remember, sitting in a restaurant in Hong Kong in 1990, having dinner with business friends, when the dulcet tones of a mobile 'phone were heard and about 300 people rushed to answer their 'phone thinking the call was for them, and almost in unison, uttered the word "why-ee", which is "hello" in Cantonese.

Another difficulty is the language – as Cantonese is not spoken away from the south and Mandarin generally not understood in Hong Kong.

Company law in Hong Kong allows for a wide range of commercial activity. There are no restrictions on the type or nature of activity, taxes are low and the tax system easy to use.

The Invest Hong Kong (InvestHK) organisation is a government department and provides excellent service for companies looking to open an office or invest in Hong Kong.

Currently, more than 800 foreign businesses have set up their regional headquarters in Hong Kong and obviously use it as a staging post for entry into China.

Contraband
Smuggling between China and Hong Kong has been going on for centuries, although Beijing did try to clamp down on it in 1998, particularly between Hong Kong and Guangzhou. The affect of smuggling on the economy has, in past times, distorted trade flows and figures.

Be aware of the 'grey channels' and the role of 'converters' when it comes to trading between Hong Kong and China, but it would be foolhardy to base any business prospects in China on continued smuggling activities.

Legal Issues
Since accession to WTO, the whole commercial system is changing in China, albeit slowly, and it will take a long time for anything radical to be noticed.

Within the law system in China, three national laws govern the general commercial framework:

• The 1986 General Principles of Civil Law

• The 1993 Company Law

• The 2000 Contract Law

Although these are national laws, they are interpreted differently at regional levels and therefore, it is important to check and understand how they will apply to where you intend setting up your business.

There are many laws dealing with foreign trade and the establishment of representative offices and foreign investment enterprises (FIEs) such as WOFEs, EJVs and CJVs.

Exporters dealing with foreign companies are commonly able to contract under international conditions so that the particular challenges of understanding the Chinese legal framework do not apply.

The situation in Hong Kong is somewhat easier and less complicated. Hong Kong's future will continue to be guided by the Basic Law which guarantees a high degree of autonomy under the principles of 'One Country, Two Systems" and "Hong Kong people running Hong Kong". The success in implementing this unique system has been recognised internationally. The legal and judicial systems have been maintained. The common law continues to apply.

And Also:
A respectful business colleague once said, 'There are three important things to do in export, particularly if you are setting up an overseas operation for the first time. They are: VISIT, VISIT and keep on VISITING.'

7

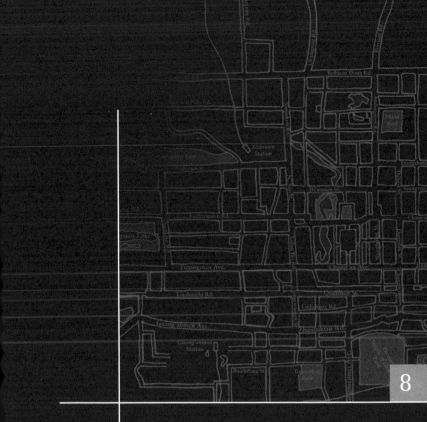

8

Beijing

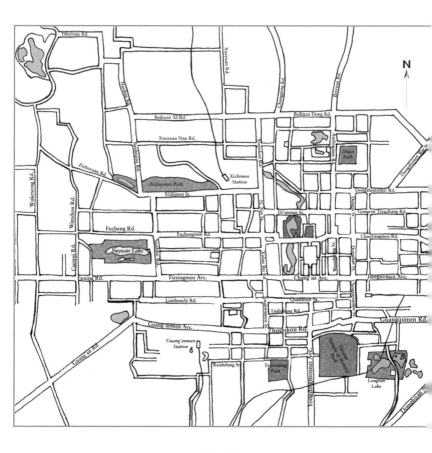

Beijing

Overview

Like many capital cities around the world, Beijing is not truly symbolic of the country it represents.

New York could not be said to represent the cultures and diversity of the USA and, likewise, London is not England. The main cities of a majority of countries are too cosmopolitan in their character to show what life is really like outside the constraints and influences that being a capital city entails.

Beijing is the seat of government in, and for, the whole of China. It is where the ministries are housed and where decisions at a national and political level are taken.

The individual provinces are autonomous, to a degree, but Beijing still wields the big stick when it comes to national matters.

Hong Kong is also autonomous and self governing, with Tung Chee hwa being the Chief Executive of the local government. In 2002, he was re-elected, unopposed, to the post for a further five years by a committee of 800 in Hong Kong, after Beijing had endorsed him.

8

Within the political community of Hong Kong, there is a movement towards full democracy by 2007, but this is contrary to the perception of the future, as portrayed by those in power in Beijing. As such, this is the source of a growing feeling of dissention by pro-democracy movements in Hong Kong. It also has its own autonomous municipal government, headed by the Mayor of Beijing. The Mayor is an influential figure and his office plays an important role in developing the infrastructure of the municipality. A quarter of the city's population is employed in the administrative sector.

Over the last millennium, Beijing has changed its name many times. Beijing or Peking or Peiping, or even Beiping, as it was sometimes spelt, was originally known as Yanjing (capital of Yan) back in the 10th century, during the period of the Liao dynasty.

Having breached the Great Wall of China in 1215 AD, Genghis Khan virtually destroyed the city of Yanjing and from the ashes the new city of Dadu was created. This period also saw the rise of the Yuan dynasty, 1215 to 1368 AD.

During the Ming dynasty, the city was re-named Peiping (or Beiping), meaning 'Northern Peace' though the capital of China was located in Nanjing at that time.

In the early part of the 15th century, the seat of government shifted back to Peiping and it was re-named Beijing (Northern Capital).

The city centre is laid out in a grid system according to ancient Feng Shui principles, or geomancy. The Beijing skyline has changed dramatically since the early 1990s, with the appearance of vast commercial developments, hotel complexes, shopping plazas and office blocks, all to accommodate and serve the increasing demands and expectations of the more affluent Chinese middle class, and the growing numbers of foreign investors settling in the city. Luxury hotels have sprung up to cope with the increasing demand from business visitors and tourists.

There are always casualties in the cause for progress and advancement. In Beijing, one casualty is the traditional housing areas surrounding the *hutongs* or back lanes. The *hutong* was once the centre of life for the local population, but they, and the communal way of life that goes with them, are threatened by urban redevelopment. The government policy is to move citizens to better quality housing and it has funded the construction of high-rise, high-density, apartment blocks to accommodate low income families. The requirement for more land for the hosting of the 2008 Olympic Games is adding to the pressure.

Weather

Located in the north of China, Beijing has four seasons similar to those of the UK or northern US. The winters are very cold and relatively dry and the summers can be hot and sticky, with high humidity. Autumn is generally a good time to visit as it is more temperate – although it is prone to rain. Spring is also a pleasant time to visit, when the trees are in bloom and the ravages of winter have passed, but sandstorms originating from the Gobi Desert region sometimes occur.

Getting Around in Beijing

For the business visitor, the easiest and most efficient way of getting around Beijing is by taxi which are always plentiful outside hotels or on the street. Always carry a note of your destination written in Chinese for the taxi driver to identify, but don't forget, the taxi driver may not be literate and able to understand even the clearest of written characters. If in doubt, ask the hotel doorman or porter to read the address and tell the taxi driver where you need to go. Be prepared to be taken for a ride, literally, by the taxi driver and it helps to have a map of Beijing with your destination address marked, just to give the impression you know where you want to go, even if you haven't the faintest idea. If the taxi doesn't have a meter, negotiate the price first before you set off, or get the hotel doorman to do this on your behalf.

The Beijing Metro system is very efficient, cheap and also being expanded to cope with the influx of additional visitors, both business and tourists and also for the Olympic Games in 2008. The locals are getting used to travelling underground, thus avoiding the traffic jams that are getting worse as the car population increases. Obviously, if travelling to an appointment by Metro, you need to know the station where to alight and also the right exit to emerge from, otherwise it could be difficult to find your desired location.

Once you are at your destination, don't forget, you have to find your way back or the way to your next appointment, so, if in doubt, ask for help and directions at the office you are leaving as that could save you a lot of time and frustration.

The hire car industry in Beijing is increasing and improving but ensure you have a valid international driving licence. Also, you have to be aware that unescorted travel by foreigners outside of Beijing is still frowned upon by the authorities. Checking into a hotel outside of the capital will alert them to your presence, as the receptionist will need to take a photocopy of your passport, and questions will no doubt be asked of you.

Treasures – a Brief Insight

Beijing is a veritable treasure house for those interested in the humanity of any culture, and Chinese history presents a fascinating story – although coping with the dates of the dynasties can be somewhat confusing.

8

The Cultural Revolution between 1966 and 1976 took its toll on many of the historic treasures throughout China, but careful restoration has taken place over the years to bring them back to their former glory. Everything seems to be as it was, or as the authorities would like you to believe it was, in previous times.

Groups of foreign tourists are much in evidence wherever you go around the city, as are the inevitable and perennial, scruffily dressed salesman of postcards and other such tacky ephemera, so typical of any major tourist attraction, no matter where you may be in the world.

A brief insight into typical major attractions in Beijing are as follows:

The Great Wall of China. Most tours take you to see the Wall at Badaling but this has become far too commercial. A better place to visit and marvel at the splendour of its construction is Mutianyu, which is about 75 miles (125 km) from Beijing. There is a cable car at this location to avoid the steep climb, and it is where VIP visitors are usually taken, rather than to Badaling. If you have local friends, ask them to hire a car or small minibus for you, complete with driver and interpreter, who will take you for a days' tour to the Great Wall, the **Ming Tombs** and other sights, at a reasonable price. That way, you miss out on the crowds and crass commercialism by having locals to look after your interests.

The Forbidden City, or Imperial Palace, is located adjacent to Tiananmen Square and you will need all the time in the world to visit, if you are to do it justice. A fleeting visit will not come anywhere close to appreciating and understanding the beauty and history of this splendid city within a city. The Forbidden City is where Emperors of China used to live and which only a few foreigners had ever penetrated until the Boxer Rebellion brought European and United States troops to Peking in 1900. It was previously home to two dynasties of emperors, the Ming and the Qing, and neither occupants strayed from within its walls unless it was imperative. The Forbidden City is based upon geomantic design on a north–south axis and all important buildings within the city face south, primarily to avoid the Siberian winds in the winter months or the marauding enemies from the Mongolian north. During the dynastic periods of Ming and Qing, the city was also the centre of the religious movements in China, although many of the shrines and temples relating to Dao, Buddha and Lama, as well as mosques and churches, were damaged or destroyed during the Cultural Revolution (1966 – 1976), or had been turned into schools or factories after the end of the Chinese Civil War in 1949.

The area of the Forbidden City is approx 170 acres, or 70 hectares, and it is estimated that, at one time, somewhere between 8,000 to 10,000 people lived and worked within its confines. The whole area of the city is surrounded by a wide moat and walls more than 30 feet (10 meters) high with the main entrance gate, Wumen (Meridian Gate) on the south, overlooking Tiananmen Square. The journey through the Forbidden City is one that cannot be hurried and shoulder carrying cassette tapes can be hired, with commentary by Peter Ustinov or Roger Moore, to guide you through the many facets, treasures and historical references that would otherwise escape the cursory or uninformed visitor.

8

When you eventually reach the exit at the northern gate, Shenwumen (Gate of Divine Prowess), you will see across the street, from where the multitude of tourists, coaches are parked, the park and hill of **Jing Shan**. This is also known as Coal Hill and Prospect Hill. From the top of Jing Shan, the best views can be had of the Forbidden City and the five pavilions that dominate the hill. It is said that the hill was constructed by the soil excavated from the palace moats when they were dug in the 15th century. It was also maintained that coal seams existed beneath the hill, hence one of the names given to the hill. The five peaked hill also provided the emperors with a 'prospect' (view), from which they could enjoy the scope and beauty of their enclave, and that is how the other name came about.

When you are in **Tiananmen Square**, it is virtually impossible to escape the presence of Mao Zedong. A huge portrait of Mao adorns the south side gate on to Tiananmen Square and his mausoleum is a large building and a 'must' for tourists to visit. The embalmed body of Mao lies in state in a rose-coloured, glass enclosure and people from all over China pay homage and respect to their revered leader. Many tourists also visit the mausoleum out of morbid curiosity. Outside the mausoleum, socialism, capitalism and total tackiness go hand in hand as visitors are directed through a small bazaar selling busts of Chairman Mao, badges and many other items of a 'must have' nature. The latest fashion accessory is a wrist watch, depicting Chairman Mao on the watch face, and his left arm replaces the second hand and waves in time with each second. It is good, but perhaps sad to admit, but my 'Mao' watch keeps perfect time!

On 1st October 1949 Mao Zedong, in his position as Chairman of the Chinese Communist Party (CCP), proclaimed the founding of the People's Republic of China (PRC) from the balcony of Tiananmen, or the Gate of Heavenly Peace. This gate, with its giant portrait of Chairman Mao, is a familiar backdrop in images of the capital of China. It is the proper entrance into the Imperial City but not the tourist entrance to the Forbidden City, that is close by. The square itself is huge, covering an area of about 40 hectares and in the 1960s it was enlarged from about 11 hectares, creating room for about 1 million people. In 1989, Tiananmen Square acquired its own place in history when the government used the army to quell the students' pro-democracy demonstrations, resulting in untold deaths and re-criminations. The image of a lonely student, standing in front of an army tank whilst holding a carrier bag, is one that will continue to be shown by the media around the world, whenever the situation arises.

Also in Tiananmen Square is **The Great Hall of the People**, and each year, in March, China's parliament meets to consider the decisions of the Politburo and Central Committee with great care, before giving them their unanimous approval. The building is huge and in 1996 I had the pleasure of seeing inside the Great Hall as part of a large UK Trade Mission, led by Michael Heseltine, who at that time was Deputy Prime Minister in the UK Government.

We assembled in the Great Hall for a group photograph, which included Li Peng, the Chinese Premier, and manyother important dignitaries of that period.

The walls were clad in the most beautiful silk hangings depicting typical Chinese scenes and the furniture, although sparce, was of museum quality.

8

The Temple of Heaven is another marvel to behold in Beijing. The centre piece of this complex is Qinian Dian, the Hall of Prayer for Good Harvests. This building, being of timber construction, was built without the use of a single nail and is a magnificent example of Chinese religious architecture and ingenuity. The three levels of its roof arc clad in deep blue tiles that symbolise the colour of heaven. There are so many superlatives and traditions attached to this building, and the park in which it is set, that it is impossible to do it justice by description. The building itself is central within an area of 670 acres (270 hectares) and in the south of the park lies the Hianqiutan, Altar of Heaven, and the Echo Wall, which is renowned for its acoustic qualities. The Hianqiutan is made of white marble and the dimensions and means of constructing such a perfectly symmetrical terrace are incredible, when you consider that building took place during the Ming dynasty, without the assistance of modern construction methods, surveying equipment and machinery.

The list of places of interest to visit and enjoy in Beijing is endless, and as a business visitor it is unlikely that you will ever get to see them all, unless your plans are to visit on a regular basis or, indeed, make Beijing your base. Beijing has a unique history, as a city of grace and style: that so lavishly grew and enjoyed special status under the auspices of the Chinese Communist Party. The Cultural Revolution, 1966 – 1976, made its mark on the Chinese with books, paintings, poetry and music all consumed by flames by the ever-present, and fanatical Red Guards. Chairman Mao's *Little Red Book* was the all-embracing ideology of the age, and those old enough will recall the TV news reports of masses of Chinese waving their Little Red Books in defiance of western culture and influence.

Understandably, the Chinese are extremely proud of their culture and history, but obviously now have need of the influences, technology and support from outside, if they are to survive and grow in what is rapidly becoming a vast global market and economy. The fact that so many foreign companies are investing and setting up substantial operations in China, not just for the short term, but indefinitely, strengthens the argument for being there, and for being an important factor in the expansion of a country that has so much to offer.

8

Schooling

With the ever-increasing expansion of China through foreign investment, the numbers of expatriate employees working in China, and in particular Beijing, is also expanding, and in a majority of cases these 'expats' are there on a family contract, although many will be on a bachelor status.

The 'expat' families require education for their offspring plus recreational facilities and, as a result, the number of international schools has increased to cope with the demand, although with the interest shown in China by foreign investors, it is likely the demand will outstrip the supply. The advice is: get in early if you are planning to move to Beijing on a family contract.

In Beijing there are currently about 20 international schools, catering for children from 3 years up to 18 years of age, and for English speaking children, Beijing has four main international schools with internationally recognised curricular and tests carried out equivalent to SATS. Children with special needs are catered for as well, so, in theory, children, and their parents, should be able to adapt to this new and interesting way of life, without experiencing too many problems.

However, none of this comes free; the cost of education is expensive and no doubt will increase as demand escalates. It is perhaps not too obvious to state that the most well resourced schools are located in the large cities and areas of economic growth.

For the English-speaking schools in Beijing, there are some websites that might be useful for obtaining further information to help with your thoughts on the subject:

International School of Beijing (ISB)
Website: [www.isb.bj.edu.cn]

Western Academy of Beijing (WAB)
Website: [www.wab.edu]

Yew Chung Beijing International School (BIS)
Website:
[www.ycef.com/en/Beijing_yewchung_school/index.htm]

Beijing International School of Singapore (BISS)
Website: [www.biss.com.cn]

In addition to the above, there is also:

Montessori School of Beijing (MSB)
Website: [www.montessoribj.com]

A further useful contact for those planning to become an expat in China is Expatriate Essentials. The website is [www.expatessentials.com]

Within all of these schools, there is a wide range of curricula available, including British, American, Montessori and International Baccalaureate.

Food and Culture

As in most cities, cafés and restaurants come and go but here are some of the places worth visiting at the time of writing:

One of the most famous haunts in Beijing is the **Hard Rock Café,** located in the west wing of the Landmark Towers building. It is huge inside and is the place to be seen. The usual Hard Rock formula applies and live bands and loud music feature on most evenings.

The bar in the **Jianguo Hotel** on Jianguomenwai Dajie, which is part of the main avenue between the China World Trade Centre and Tiananmen Square, is a well known watering hole for expats, and is commonly known as **Charlie's Bar**. In the evenings there is live music, with decent beers and a good, friendly atmosphere.

Karaoke bars abound in Beijing, but be careful about the price of drinks, especially if you are on your own, as these places have fluctuating price lists to suit the nationality of the clientele.

The **Beijing Opera** is a renowned cultural feature in the city, but tends nowadays to be tourist-orientated, with opera costumes and full facial makeup provided for those brave enough to have their photo taken to record the event.

If classical music is your scene, European and Chinese concerts can be enjoyed at either the **Beijing Concert Hall** (tel 601 8092) or at the **Central Music Conservatory** (tel 605 3531). There are also concerts, especially on a Sunday afternoon, in the large lobby of the **China World Hotel,** where the atmosphere is relaxed. **The Swissôtel** (tel 501 2288) also have concerts in their lobby.

8

8

Minstrel/Minister

Several years ago, I was invited for dinner by my local Beijing contacts and taken to a Mongolian Hotpot restaurant. As we were preparing to dine, the owner of the restaurant, who was a good friend of my host, appeared and sat at our table. The Hotpot is similar to a Western fondue where you cook your own strips of meat, fish, vegetables in hot oil. I learnt that the owner of the restaurant was not only a senior ministry official in Beijing, but also a leading singer with the Beijing Opera. He re-appeared a short while later, clad in a beautiful Chinese cloak and headdress, carrying a small musical instrument. He then proceeded to give us a rendition of several well known (at least well known to my hosts) songs, and his performance lasted nearly half an hour. Whilst I didn't have a clue of what he was singing about, he had a magnificent voice and it made for an evening to be remembered. A bit like a Chinese Pavarotti, and similar in stature!

Beijing Zoo has its own restaurant (Binfengtan) offering such delights, and seasonal delicacies as pheasant, turtles, frogs, monkey, snake, deer, etc.

The choice of food in Beijing is not only multi-national but also multi-provincial as well. There are restaurants specialising in Imperial Food, Cantonese, Chaozhou, Hunan, Sichuan and Jiaozi cuisines. There are a multitude of European food restaurants, mainly situated in the major hotels, plus a selection of Asian food restaurants, offering Indian, Indonesian, Malay, Korean, Thai, Vietnamese and Japanese menus. If your taste buds need a further change, Russian, Brazilian and Mexican restaurants are also in evidence, plus of course the regular 'fast food' outlets, which are easily recognised by their familiar signs, if you really need to slob out for a cheap meal with a familiar flavour.

Shopping
Being on a business visit doesn't always allow time for serious shopping.

In Beijing, the **Friendship Store** on Jianguomenwai is a good place to start. It is large and stocks tourist trinkets, every day items such as food, wines, drinks, coffee, clothes and high fashion items, jewellery, watches, electrical goods, Chinese medicines, cooking utensils, luxury goods, books, in fact you name it, you will probably find it!

The main street of **Jianguomenwai**, which changes its name to Dongchang'an Jie, runs between the China World Trade Centre (CWTC) and Tiananmen Square, and is a trek in itself. It doesn't look too far on the map, but it can take two hours or more to walk, that is of course, allowing for re-fuelling stops in hotel bars or street cafés en route. There are many excellent stores to visit, not only in the main street, but also the side streets you aspire to during your traverse. If walking from the CWTC, it is best to stay on the right hand side of the road, as the choice seems to be greater.

Just before the Beijing Hotel is the area of **Wangfujing**, a popular area with locals and tourists.

The area of **Liulichang** is renowned for its selection of antique shops, but don't be fooled by the apparent age of the goods on display, as most are fakes. Another 'antique' market is Hongqiao, but again, beware of bargains.

In **Sanlitun**, you will find the Kempinski Hotel, which incorporates the Lufthansa Centre, and the Great Wall Sheraton Hotel is close by. This neighbourhood has some of the more upmarket stores with prices to match.

An area originally known as Silk Street, is now **Dazhalan**, and has an interesting collection of department stores, silk shops, Chinese herbal medicine emporiums, theatres, etc.

If you are looking for computer equipment, software or similar goods, then head for **Zhongguancun** as it has the best selection of computer shops in Beijing. Two things to be wary of are pirated goods and virus infected products.

8

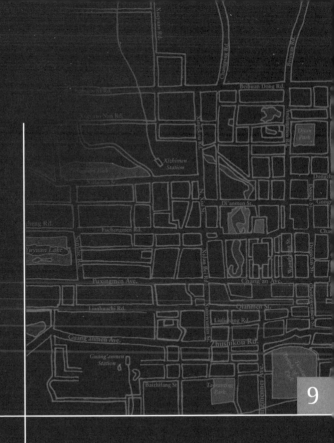

9

other major cities

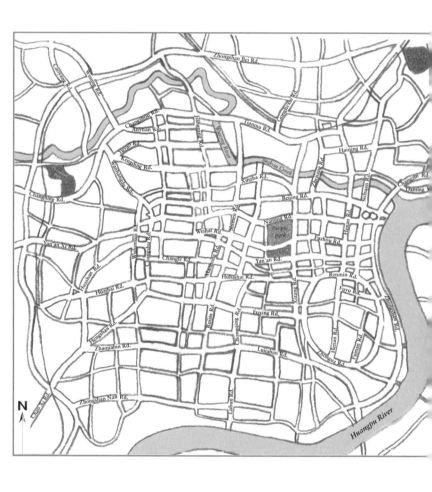

Shanghai

This chapter covers other cities in China where you might consider locating your business.

Shanghai

Shanghai is the sixth most populous city in the world, and, despite not being the capital of China, it is larger than Beijing in area, covering about 5,800 square kilometers. The population fluctuates, with a recognised number of inhabitants placed at 13 million in 2001 but a fluctuating population of about 3 million migrant workers, a majority of whom work on the ever increasing number of construction sites springing up in this rapidly developing and expanding city.

Weather

The climate here is moderate, being in the sub-tropical zone between the hot and humid south and the dry and cold north. Fine weather can usually be guaranteed between spring and autumn but cold weather can be expected in winter with temperatures dropping to below 5°C.

Potted History

It was after the Opium Wars that the British moved into Shanghai under the Treaty of Nanking in 1842, and the French were close behind. The 'concessions' that followed allowed the trade in opium to continue undisturbed and these two nations were soon in competition with Italians, Japanese, Germans and Americans. These nations left their mark on the city's architecture, as enclaves were created to accommodate these foreign traders. They also were allowed to reside under their own national laws, policed by their own security forces with indefinite leases being granted.

The city grew in size and prospered and was often referred to as the Paris of the East. In the 1920s and 1930s, it was a smart, cosmopolitan and fashionable city, but drugs and prostitution were significant industries of their time and many fortunes were made and lost. The Chinese Communist Party (CCP) was formed in 1921 and it was driven underground in Shanghai after the brutal massacre of hundreds of strikers in 1927.

Nevertheless, the CCP continued with its doctrines and after the Communist take-over in 1949, and the

9

formation of The People's Republic of China (PRC), Shanghai remained a centre of radicalism. Chairman Mao launched the Great Proletarian Cultural Revolution from Shanghai in 1966, aided by his wife Jian Qing, after being stifled by bureaucracy in Beijing. After Mao's death, Shanghai was the last stronghold of the Gang of Four in their struggle for succession, although their planned coup never materialised.

Shanghai continues to breed leaders: President Jiang Zemin and Premier Zhu Rongji, were both former Mayors of Shanghai.

Transport and Logistics
Shanghai started off as a fishing village and it wasn't until the 13th century that it attained any form of independent status.

The city grew through its position as a flourishing trading port and it still retains its place as a major shipping destination for both imports and exports. In 2001, Shanghai handled about 30 per cent of China's sea trade, and it is interesting to note that Shanghai is twinned with the City of Liverpool in the UK, another major port with a long and substantial trading history.

Situated almost equidistant between Beijing and Guangzhon on the Chinese eastern seaboard of the East China Sea and to the east of the Yangtse Delta, Shanghai controls the entrance to the Chang Jiang, or Yangtze River, China's principal inland waterway.

Shanghai also straddles the Huangpu River, which was a main artery for merchant vessels, barges, ferry boats, and all the craft that through the centuries have plied their trade in a very cosmopolitan and free thinking society.

The city is also the intermediate terminal for the two major railway lines in China; Beijing – Shanghai and Shanghai – Guangzhou (Canton).

There are two international airports located in Shanghai, the original being HongQiao, followed by the more recently constructed, Pudong, the first phase of which opened for traffic in 1999.

Most international flights are being concentrated into the airport at Pudong, which is about 40 kms from the Shanghai's city centre. It is, however, more ideally

9

situated for the main industrial areas of Pudong (East Shanghai) and Puxi (West Shanghai). Pudong International Airport has the capacity to handle 30 million passengers per year and up to 750,000 tonnes of freight per annum.

With the increasing infrastructural demands, Shanghai is also an important road transport hub and with the burgeoning numbers of foreign investors setting up business in Shanghai, the need for good, reliable and cost effective distribution services is an essential requirement for choosing Shanghai as your base.

Education

Since those heady days of political infighting and economic turmoil, Shanghai has evolved into a centre of academia and learning and is almost unequalled in China; there are currently more than 50 colleges and universities, with over 120,000 students. There are a number of international schools in Shanghai, catering for the children of foreign employees settling in China and expecting curricula of a standard equal to their home country.

9

In 2002, the Nord Anglia Education Group opened its first school in Shanghai, The British International School. It is an independent school, offering education for boys and girls aged from 3 to 18 years. The UK contact number for more information is +44 161 491 8482.

Industries

Since the early 1990s, the economy of Shanghai has shown a continual rise in fortunes, with the IT and finance sectors being the strongest, with the insurance sector also showing steady growth.

Shanghai is a major manufacturing centre, with its prime 'pillar' industries being:

- Automotive

- Information

- Iron & Steel

- Chemicals

- Household Appliances

- Power Equipment and Machinery

Other industries in Shanghai include, telecommunications, micro-electronics, computers, textiles, medicines, pharmaceuticals, building materials, light industry products, machinery, electronics, bio-tech and environmental protection and petrochemicals.

The service industry is also developing fast, as is the market for consumer goods.

Stocks & Shares

The Shanghai Stock Exchange was established in 1990 and now boasts more than 500 quoted companies. In 2001, the opening of the B share market led to a significant interest in the Stock Market by domestic investors, increasing the desire of the growing 'middle classes' to spend their disposable income on a different form of gambling.

Pudong (East Shanghai)

The New Pudong Area is virtually a self contained 'city' in itself. It has a population of about 1.5 million, an area larger than Singapore, about 522 square kilometers, and is sandwiched between the Huangpu River to the east and the estuary of the Yangtze River to the south west.

Within the developed area of Pudong, there are currently four key sub-zones, which are:

● Lujiazui Financial and Trade Zone

● Jinqiao Export Processing Zone

● Waigaoqiao Free Trade Zone

● Zhangjiang Hi-Tech Park

In the early 1990s, the land around Pudong was given over almost entirely to agriculture but now Foreign Investment is an important part of the industrial and economic development of the area.

When I visited Shanghai in 1996 on the Heseltine Trade Mission we were taken to Pudong to see the projected plans and model for its development, and this was considered, at the time, to be a hugely ambitious programme. However, in many respects, it has taken shape despite the portents of doom at the time, and the economic crisis in the region in 1997/98. The Pudong area is projected to be the driving force for the overall development of the Yangtze River Delta region, an area totaling about 500,000 square kilometres.

The number of well known, multinational companies that have set up business in Pudong is to large to list.

Puxi (West Shanghai)

Puxi and Pudong are divided by the Huangpu River and it is in Puxi where the local government is situated. The two areas are connected by bridges and tunnels so day to day communication is not a problem, apart from the usual traffic jams.

The Mayor of Shanghai commands tremendous respect and it is a highly influential position, as the names and high ranking positions of previous incumbents will testify.

Many well known multi-national companies have chosen Puxi to set up their offices and businesses in, and despite a push from local government to move established operations to Pudong, many firms have resisted but, as older accommodation blocks are no longer allowed expansion approval, residents are gradually relocated to Pudong.

9

Redevelopment

When I visited Shanghai in 2001, as a member of another UK Government Minister-led Trade Mission, part of our programme included a visit to a large redevelopment project in the heart of Shanghai. This was known as Xintiandi (literally 'New Heaven and Earth'). It was the first phase of the 52 hectare, US$3.2 billion, Tiapingqiao (Tie-ping-chow) Redevelopment project. It involved the preservation and transformation of blocks of the historic Longtangs (flagstone alleys) and the unique Shikumen (stone framed gate houses), which were synonymous of the architectural styles of the past.

The fact this area was also located within the prestigious commercial centre of Shanghai also gave the project a significantly high profile as much of these areas had previously been demolished and lost forever.

Originally built in the 19th and 20th centuries, Longtangs were walled neighbourhoods lined by rows of two and three storey enclosed courtyard dwellings with Shikumen as entrances to the houses. Since most of the

Shikumen houses were built by foreign companies, in the foreign concessions at that time, they had become a symbol of East meeting West.

The heavy black wooden front doors of the Shikumen houses were framed by elaborately sculpted lintels, decorated with either Chinese characters or rococo motifs. Because of this fusion of both Chinese and Western elements, the Shikumen is distinctly Shanghainese.

According to the business plan for the redevelopment, one of the purposes of Xintiandi was to make Shanghai a world class city without foregoing the beauty of nature and the history of the municipality.

The redevelopment comprised a high quality business and living environment, a 40,000 square metres park featuring a 10,000 square metres man-made lake. Adjacent to the park is Corporate Avenue, which will cater for the needs of multi-national organisations by the provision of Grade A offices. Close by are high quality residential dwellings and precinct, with all the usual amenities.

9

Ding Dong

The Customs House, on the Bund in Shanghai, has a clock known as "Big Ching".

The clock was supplied and installed in 1930 by the oldest tower clock maker in the world, a company called J.B. Joyce & Company, founded in 1690, from Whitchurch, Shropshire, England and still keeps perfect time.

Originally, the clock had a Westminster chime, striking every 15 minutes, just like Big Ben at the Houses of Parliament in London, but office workers in the vicinity were disturbed by the constant sound of the chimes, so now it only strikes the hour and the half hour.

A flavour of Shanghai

Shanghai does not profess to be a 'tourist' city, but it does have many attractions and generally speaking, **the Bund,** fronting onto the Huangpu River is where most visitors gravitate for their 'shot' of Shanghainese culture.

The Bund, so named by the British after the Opium Wars, is actually taken from the Indian word, *bund*, meaning embankment. It was here, that the Bund was occupied by European, American and Japanese banks, trading house, hotels, clubs of various, and dubious, occupants, and foreign consulates.

By night, the buildings on the Bund are well lit and it is quite a spectacular sight to behold, and a famous image from many guide books on the region. Amongst these buildings is the well known **Peace Hotel**, which in its heyday during the 1930s, was the place to stay, and many famous, and infamous, characters from recent history have slept within its walls. Originally built by Victor Sassoon, allegedly from the profits of his trade in opium, the Peace Hotel is on the list of 'must see' attractions, as is the Jazz Band that performs there on a nightly basis. My own impression of the Jazz Band is one of the living dead! You have to see both the hotel and its band to appreciate my comments. Although, I must say, the band does liven up as the evening draws to a close.

9

If you fancy a change from the multitude of excellent local restaurants in Shanghai, I can suggest a visit to **Irenes Thai** Restaurant at 263 Tong Re Road, (tel 6247 3579), but you will need to book in advance as it is always busy. As the name suggests, Thai food is the specialty but you have to appreciate spicy cuisine to do it justice.

After your meal, the **Cotton Club** at 1428 HuaiHai Road (tel 6437 7110) is a good place to wind down, enjoy decent live music in a relaxed atmosphere and have a nightcap at the end of a busy day.

Shanghai sometimes boasts having the busiest street in the world. **Nanjing Lu** is principally the main thoroughfare through the city, and is where all the new department stores and old established shops are comfortable neighbours. In this street, which is busy all day and well into the night, every day and night without exception, everything imaginable can be bought. It always seems to be at its best at night, when the neon signs lining the busy street create a unique atmosphere and everyone is out, looking for bargains, window shopping or just to be seen.

One of the inescapable sights in Shanghai is the **Shanghai Minzhu**, otherwise known as Oriental Pearl TV Tower, located in the Pudong area and on the banks of the Huangpu River. Lifts (elevators) will whisk you to the top for a bird's eye view of Shanghai. The tower is one of the sights of the city and it looks just like a space ship, ready to launch at any minute. By night, it looks even more daunting.

Shanghai is different from other Chinese cities. The people are more cosmopolitan, they have their own, specific dialect, their food is different, they are more fashionable and indeed, possibly more worldly as a result of contact with 'outside' cultures over the past 150 years or so, and a heritage of being a trading city.

Guangzhou – Guangdong Province

Guangzhou is located in the heart of the **Pearl River Delta** region, and is also the political and economic centre, and capital, of Guangdong Province, China's commercial powerhouse. The official population of Guangdong Province is more than 71 million and it has the largest number of foreign invested enterprises in China.

The city of Guangzhou, formerly known as Canton, is also seen as the entrepreneurial capital of China and sits comfortably within an affluent economic region, which includes Hong Kong, Shenzhen, Zhuhai and Macau.

The Pearl River has seen many of the West's historical encounters and battles with China and between 1757 to 1842, it was the only Chinese port open to foreign trading vessels. In 1839, the Chinese ordered the confiscation of about 20,000 chests containing opium and this, in turn led to military intervention by Britain and the First Opium War in the early 1840s, resulting in the Treaty of Nanking in 1842 and the 'concessions' that went with the treaty.

Today, Guangzhou Municipality comprises 10 districts and two county level cities, Zengcheng and Conghua, covering a total area of nearly 7,500 square kilometers.

In 2001, the registered population was about 10 million and on an average day, nearly 1.9 million people commute into Guangzhou from surrounding areas.

The city, being situated on the Pearl River, has a long history as a trading port and also has had an open mind towards the influences of the outside world. Being geographically close to Hong Kong, Guangzhou and other cities to the south, such as Dong Guan, and more typically Shenzhen, had an even greater influence almost thrust upon them during the emerging 1980s. This was the satellite dish and the TV stations and channels transmitted therefrom. These images of life in the Western world were an obvious attraction to the Cantonese, and perhaps that is why this province is reputedly the original home of a majority of overseas Chinese. Having seen on TV what life outside could be like, they had to escape to the West, as many did. It was once said to me that Beijing is too far away, too remote, to seriously affect the thoughts and actions of the Cantonese. When you consider that, even in these days of modern travel, it still takes about three and a half hours to fly from Guangzhou to Beijing, and it also takes more than 24 hours to complete the same journey by train, you can then understand the difficulty that central government would have had in maintaining a common policy for a country the size of China.

9

The proximity to Hong Kong has been an important and significant factor in the growth of Guangzhou and other cities within Guangdong province. Investment from Hong Kong has been concentrated largely in Guangdong where industrial investment, primarily outward processing arrangements, still predominates. Nevertheless, over the years, Hong Kong businessmen have extended the scope of their investment from industrial processing to other sectors such as hotels and tourist related services, real estate, retail trade, infrastructural construction and various business and communications services.

It should not be forgotten that many of the Hong Kong businessmen, or their families, originate from Guangdong province and, apart from the obvious financial benefits, there is a certain kudos to displaying your wealth and business acumen, by being even more successful in your home town.

In 2001, the economy of Guangzhou grew by 12.7%, which is greater than the growth of China as a whole, and higher than either Beijing or Shanghai.

The rise in urban disposable income during 2001 resulted in increased household spending on housing, cars and education. This spending has been seen as bucking the trend and bolstering the economic trend during a period of global economic slowdown.

The forecast for Guangdong province is for steady growth with a continuing emphasis on modernisation and new infrastructure projects such as the Guangzhou Metro extension, port expansion, and expressway projects. There are also plans to create the **Nansha Development Zone**, which will be Guangzhou's answer to the Pudong Zone in Shanghai. These plans include the development of a 22-square kilometre district to include a deep water port, ship building and steel plants, plus a high technology zone. Nansha is seen by Guangzhou as central to its plans to develop the region's economy and reinforce the already firm links between Hong Kong and the Eastern Pearl River Delta.

The traditional 'pillar' industries in Guangzhou are:

- Automobile Projects, such as Guangzhou–Honda sedans.

- Pearl River Steelworks project

- Relocation of Guangzhou Cement factory

- Guangzhou export processing zone.

The electronic information and high technology sectors of industry are also very important for Guangzhou and there are many plans for the expansion of these industries.

By 2002, more than 60 British companies are represented in Guangzhou and you only have to travel by car from the border with Hong Kong at Shenzhen to witness the extent of foreign investment in the 'corridor' bordering the expressway on a journey that takes about one and a half hours to reach the outskirts of Guangzhou. The companies located there are from such diverse industries as paints and chemicals, food products, banks, insurance, electrical, aero engines, power plants, oil, steel and shipping, to name just a few. These are the main multi-national organisations but there are many other smaller, less well known companies making their mark in a growth economy and rapidly developing region.

9

The Guangzhou New Baiyun Airport, located in Huadu, north of Guangzhou, and currently under construction, is due to become operational towards the end of 2003, and will be the largest, and first hub airport, in China.

It will be linked to a new expressway and an elevated Light Rail Transit (LRT) system taking arriving passengers to the Guangzhou main line railway station and also linking with Line 2 of the Guangzhou Metro. The new airport is designed to handle up to 25 million passengers and 1 million tonnes of cargo per annum.

According to the 10th Five-year Plan (2001 – 2005) for Guangdong province, the emphasis is on social and economic development with planned modernisation around the Pearl River Delta, with Guangzhou, and the province's three Special Economic Zones of Shenzhen, Zhuhai and Shantou taking the lead. Improvements to the expressways, and improving the province's electricity supply are high priorities for the province.

Dong Guan and Chang An

Situated between Guangzhou and Shenzhen is the city of Dong Guan, which is connected with the Special Economic Zone of Shenzhen. Within Dong Guan is Chang An Industrial City and this has become a very popular, although for some strange reason, less well known, area for foreign investment. By the end of the 1990's, there were nearly 1,500 foreign enterprises established in Chang An, of which 55 per cent were from Hong Kong, 305 from Taiwan, 5 per cent from Japan and the balance were described as 'others'!

The area around Chang An, and Dong Guan itself is expanding rapidly, both in terms of industrial development, but also as a second home for businessmen from Hong Kong. It has good infrastructural services, excellent hotels, elegant golf courses and country clubs, and is set within a very pleasant environment.

In logistical terms, there is the Chang An Operation Zone of Humen Port, which is classified as a Class 1 National Port, approved by the State Council. Chang An currently has three power stations, with adequate water supplies and good IDD, mobile phone, Internet and Email communication networks.

9

Shenzhen – Guangdong Province

It is interesting, reading through the tourist guide books for China, there is scant reference to Guangdong Province and in fact, in only one guide book does Shenzhen get a mention, and that is a very brief note about its proximity to Hong Kong.

Shenzhen is immediately northeast of the New Territories of Hong Kong and the first city you encounter when you cross the border from Lo Wu, on the Hong Kong side. The heavily fortified and guarded border is the Sham Chun River which, you cross over either by car or on foot, and, after the immigration formalities, you emerge into the bustling city of Shenzhen.

In the mid 1980s, Shenzhen was a small, unpretentious border town surrounded by paddy fields and the occasional water buffalo, usually harnessed to a primitive wooden plough with the farmer standing on to keep the single shear blade in the ground.

9

Shenzhen is unrecognisable from those early days. With its multitude of towering and gleaming tower blocks, wide roads and beautiful gardens and parks, large industrial areas, and bustling economy, Shenzhen has overtaken most of China's major cities, and in 2002, was ranked 4th in terms of GDP, with Shanghai, Beijing and Guangzhou, being the respective leaders.

The official population of Shenzhen is around 4 million, but like other major centres of employment, this is a movable figure with the number of migrant workers being an unknown factor.

Foreign investment in Shenzhen has been significant and whilst most investments are of a relatively small scale, the actual number of firms investing are considerable. A wide range of industries have invested in the area, with manufacturing accounting for a majority of the investments, followed by the service sector as the lesser, but growing portion. The main investors so far into Shenzhen have come from Hong Kong, Taiwan, Japan, USA and Germany but it is not known how many foreign investors are linked with those from Hong Kong, and that could be quite a number.

Although Shenzhen may outwardly resemble Hong Kong with its tower blocks, it is still very much part of the

Chinese mainland and a non-Chinese, *gwailo*, face is a rare sight on the streets.

According to official statistics, the average age in Shenzhen is just over 29 and nearly 95 per cent of the adult population and workforce has moved to Shenzhen from other Chinese provinces, in search of work and to make their fortune. It is recognised that some of the working conditions for these migrant workers are quite bad with relatively low wages, but changes are slowly being enforced as more foreign investors move in, demanding and creating better standards for their workforce.

Due to its closeness to Hong Kong, Shenzhen has become a Mecca for exhibitions, and there are more than 60 exhibitions throughout the year. In 2003, a new convention and exhibition centre will be completed with a free area of about 220,000 square meters, to house the continuing and expanding requirements from exhibitors, including building products, real estate, furniture and decorations, jewellery, electronics, household goods, toys, etc, the list just goes on and on!

Shenzhen is also the thriving centre for broadcasting and publishing industries.

The expansion of the city over the years has generated an export orientated, manufacturing culture, culminating in the second largest container port in China and a major gateway for international trade, rivalling its close neighbour, Hong Kong.

It is also a fact that all of China's largest trading provinces have established offices in Shenzhen.

The international airport to the north of Shenzhen is connected to the city by a fast expressway and there are direct connections with all of China's major cities. There are also flights to a number of overseas destinations but, generally, the international airport in Hong Kong is the preferred choice, as there are a greater number of daily flights and connections.

A Metro rail system is scheduled to open in 2005 and it is planned this will provide an improved and more efficient pedestrian, immigration checkpoint for travellers between Hong Kong and Shenzhen.

9

At present, when travelling from Hong Kong to Shenzhen on foot, you have to alight at Wo Lu, on the border, and the slowest part of the journey, particularly for *gwailos*, can be proceeding through immigration. First stop is on the Hong Kong side, then after the walk across the bridge over the Sham Chun River, you then have to pass through the Chinese immigration, and, depending upon the time of day, the crowds can be substantial, as can their shin bashing, baggage trolleys!

The general standard of living in Shenzhen is good, and getting even better. There are plenty of luxury hotels and masses of restaurants catering for all tastes and budgets. The nightlife is sophisticated and golf courses are in the ascendancy, and cheaper than courses in Hong Kong.

The weather in Shenzhen is the same as Hong Kong and also for Guangzhou, hot and sticky in the summer months and slightly cooler during the winter period.

As mentioned earlier, Shenzhen does not feature on the tourist route but it does receive many foreign tourists travelling from Hong Kong and short term coach trips are readily available from major hotels in Hong Kong. This is an easy way to get a flavour of China without too much hassle. Shenzhen also boasts miles of golden sands and is rapidly becoming one of Southern China's top holiday resorts and attractions.

More than 100 British companies have been registered with the municipal authorities and Shenzhen has developed as one of China's major high-tech areas. The location is ideal, the infrastructure and communications are good, and improving fast, and the workforce is plentiful and skilled.

CBBC have an office in Shenzhen: website: [www.cbbc.org] for further information and assistance.

Western China
The western region of China, which includes Chongqing, Sichuan, Changsha, Yunnan, Guizhou, Shaanxi, Gansu, Qinghai plus the autonomous regions of Tibet, Ningxia, Xinjiang, Inner Mongolia and Guangxi, has a combined population exceeding 365 million, and therefore cannot be ignored when it comes to an area ripe for development.

9

The region described is also the home to a wide variety of natural raw materials for developing processing industries. It is also rich in terms of energy and mineral resources that are the backbone of industrial development. The three largest explored resources of natural gas in China are located in Sichuan, Shaanxi and Xinjiang and it is calculated that this sector has tremendous potential for growth. The region is also abundant in power resources and the Chinese government has in recent years, increased investment to expand the hydropower generation capacity.

The basic infrastructure needed to encourage long term investment and sustain its growth is, however, sadly lacking and there is an urgent requirement to accelerate the development of this sector, particularly as more foreign investment companies increase their interest in the region.

Western China, particularly Chongqing, pronounced 'Choong Ching', and which means 'Double Celebration', feature regularly in economic reports and the State Council announced its four key pillars, intended to generate more specific interest and attract investors:

9

● Increased capital investment in infrastructural development

● Beneficial investment incentives

● Increased scope for foreign investment

● Investment in people

The Ministry of Communications, whose responsibility includes the planning and construction of highways in China, has, in its 10th Five-Year Plan, intentions to build eight highways in the west, which will eventually amount to 15,000 kilometers on new roadways. In addition to this, are plans to construct two major bridges and all this is part of a much larger, and grander scheme, to produce 12 main corridors on national expressways, or highways, connecting provinces and shortening travelling time between major cities throughout China. The time scale to complete the scheme is by 2020.

The shift in rural labour to the newly developing urban areas is generating a boom in demand for low cost housing, which in turn creates a need for social and environmental services, and so, the cycle of supply and demand, plus the need to attain a better life style, increases.

It seems the opportunities for foreign investment in Western China are enormous and there is a raft of key environmental and infrastructural projects open to foreign bidders.

Chongqing

Chongqing is the home and origin of one of China's most famous cuisines, Sichuan, and an even lesser known fact is that Chongqing is the largest city in China. It is located on the upper reaches of the Yangtze River and is the only municipality in Southwest China reporting directly to the central government.

Twinned with the City of Leicester in the UK, Chongqing has a population of more than 30 million.

Foreign businesses already established in Chongqing include:

● Oil companies

● Food and confectionery producers

● Pharmaceutical companies

● Construction companies and Consultants

● International banks

● International hotel chains

● Management Consultants

● Building material suppliers

and the list is continuing to expand.

The contact in Chongqing for further information is:

The British Consulate General, Commercial Section.
❑ Tel: +86 23 6381 0321; fax: +86 23 6381 0322
Email: [bcgchq@public.cta.cq.cn]

Hong Kong

Once described as 'a barren rock' more than 150 years ago, Hong Kong, or more literally 'Heung Gong' means 'Fragrant Harbour', and at one time that may have been an appropriate description of what is now one of the most vibrant, exciting and infectious business environments in the world.

The usefulness of Hong Kong Island was discovered, almost by accident, by British sailors in search of fresh drinking water, when they saw a waterfall in the hills of what is now Aberdeen. They quickly became aware of the usefulness of the deepwater harbour adjacent to the island and this soon developed into one of the finest ports in the world.

Hong Kong survives totally on its wits and business acumen as a nation of hardworking, adaptable, well educated traders and entrepreneurs, who are the bedrock of Kong Kong's productivity and creativity.

As most of the world will know, Hong Kong was handed back to China on July 1st 1997 and became a Special Administrative Region (SAR) of the People's Republic of China, after 150 years of British Administration.

Under Hong Kong's constitutional document of the Basic Law, the existing economic, legal and social system will be maintained for a further 50 years. Also, with the doctrine of 'One country, two systems', Hong Kong SAR enjoys a high degree of autonomy, except in defence and foreign affairs.

The local government of Hong Kong SAR is headed by Mr Tung Chee-hwa as Chief Executive, who was re-elected in 2002 for a further 5 year term, by a committee of 800 after being endorsed by Beijing. The committee's members were mostly from the business and professional associations in Hong Kong.

Situated at the southeastern extremity of China, and comprising 235 outlying islands, Hong Kong is ideally positioned at the centre of a rapidly developing Asia Pacific region, and is considered generally to be Asia's world city, open to visitors and investors from all parts of the globe. This position is supported by a community which values freedom, generates opportunities and rewards creativity and entrepreneurship.

As one of the world's great cosmopolitan cities, Hong Kong's continued success will increasingly depend on an ability to add value in the economic, social and cultural spheres to meet the needs of the people in Hong Kong, the Chinese mainland and the global market.

9

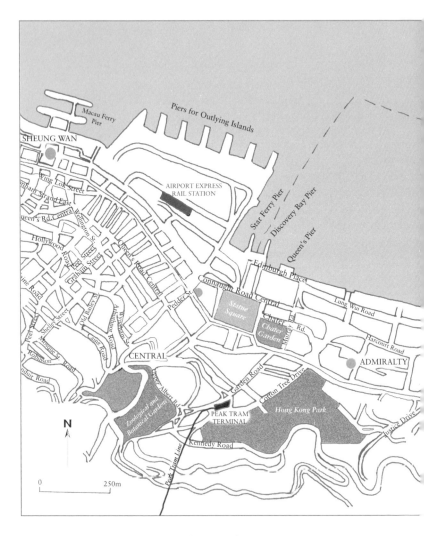

Macau Ferry Pier

Piers for Outlying Islands

SHEUNG WAN

Wing Lok Street

Bonham Strand East

Queen's Rd. Central

Hollywood Road

Peel Street

Graham Street

Wellington St.

Queen's Road Central

Jervine Road

Shelley Street

Old Bailey St.

Aberdeen Street

Wyndham St.

Cochrane Road

Mosque St.

Robinson Road

Conduit Road

Pedder St.

Pottinger Street

AIRPORT EXPRESS RAIL STATION

Star Ferry Pier

Discovery Bay Pier

Queen's Pier

Edinburgh Place

Connaught Road Central

Statue Square

Chater Garden

Lung Wui Road

Harcourt Road

Murray Rd.

Chater Rd.

ADMIRALTY

CENTRAL

Upper Albert Rd.

Zoological and Botanical Gardens

Garden Road

Cotton Tree Drive

Hong Kong Park

Justice Drive

N

PEAK TRAM TERMINAL

Peak Tram Line

Kennedy Road

0   250m

Hong Kong

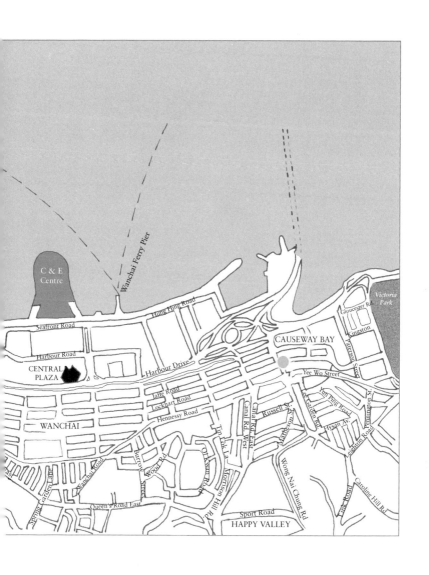

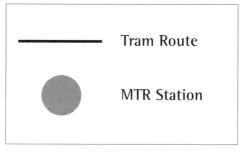

Tram Route

MTR Station

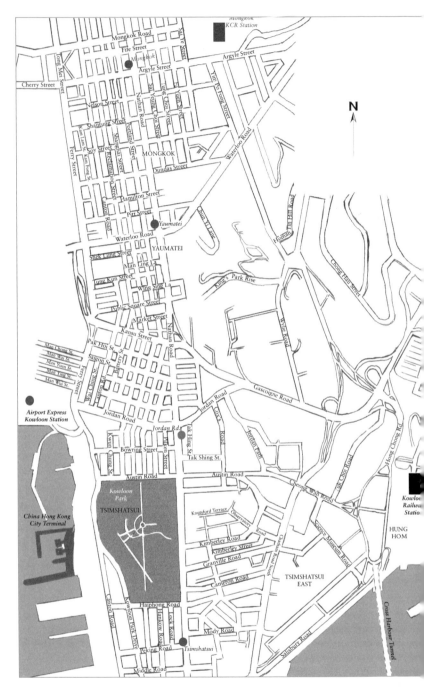

Kowloon

MTR Station

Tea

Forget about drinking coffee whilst in China as tea, or cha, is the most widely available beverage. The custom of drinking cha with friends is said to be as old as China itself. For generations, friends have welcomed and bid farewell to each other over a cup of freshly brewed Oolong, Po Lei, Jasmine, Ti Kuan Yin, or one of the many teas available as the selection is enormous. All meals are accompanied by tea, always drunk without milk, sugar or lemon,

When dining with locals, the teapot will appear as if by magic and your small cup will constantly be replenished, and it is up you whether you drink or not. Depending where you are, you will normally start with a light, green tea and finish the meal with very small, brown earthenware type cups, containing a darker tea that has an "earthy" flavour. The teapot is packed solid with the tealeaves and boiling hot water continually added to infuse before serving. The Chinese make an art of drinking tea and various types of teas have differing efficacious benefits, either for reducing cholesterol, cleansing the body or for many other diverse reasons.

There are many other flavoured teas available, such as rose, narcissus and chrysanthemum, plus of our all the medicinal 'teas' available from the medicine shops.

When drinking tea in a restaurant, you will notice that frequently, the teapot lid is lifted and placed on the top of the teapot by the handle. This is a signal to the waiter that the teapot is empty and needs replenishing with freshly boiled water. Even in the very best of restaurants, the teapot lid will invariably be tied to the handle by a short length of well used, tea stained, string.

9

Investing in the future

Hong Kong has plans to strengthen its position as Asia's world city by upgrading specific sectors of industry and consolidating its links with China and the rest of the world by:

● Investing heavily to enhance its infrastructure with a new logistics centre at the International Airport, expansion of port facilities and providing new road and rail links.

• Hong Kong Disneyland is currently under construction and scheduled to open in 2005. It will enhance Hong Kong's position as Asia's most popular tourism destination.

• An Innovation and Technology Fund of HK$ 5 billion has been established to support projects which will contribute to innovation and technological upgrading of the manufacturing and service industries.

• A Science Park is being created to nurture a world class technology community in Hong Kong.

A further range of initiatives is in place to improve the environment and also to enliven the arts and cultural scene, which include:

• Upgrading all diesel fuelled taxis with LPG powered vehicles and replacing regular diesel with the environmentally cleaner ultra-low diesel at all filling stations.

• Major programmes to upgrade sewerage and solid waste treatment.

• Development of a 40-hectare integrated arts, cultural and entertainment district in West Kowloon.

Gateway to China
Hong Kong has for a long time been considered as a gateway to the mainland of China and a business hub for the Asia Pacific region.

It has the world's busiest container port with 75% of throughput related to trade with China.

The world class financial markets in Hong Kong are an attraction to mainland companies and it is estimated that more than US$ 40 billion was raised in Hong Kong in 2001.

China's external trade and foreign direct investment (FDI) are projected to double over a period of time, as a result of accession to WTO in 2001, and much of this increased trade and investment will flow through Hong Kong.

By 2000, more than 3,000 companies had re-located to Hong Kong, establishing regional headquarters and offices in the SAR. The major types of business carried on by the regional headquarters include the wholesale/retail

9

and import/export trades. Other business services involved are accounting, advertising, legal services, finance, banking, manufacturing, transport, logistics and related industries.

Free Trade & Taxation

Hong Kong advocates and practices free trade and a free market economy with a free and liberal investment regime. There are no barriers and no discrimination against foreign investors. It encourages a freedom of capital movement, has a well established law system, with transparent regulations. It also has low and predictable taxation laws, such as:

- A low rate of tax on profits

- Only income and profits derived from Hong Kong are subject to tax

- No tax on capital gains, dividends or interest

- Generous capital allowance

- Personal tax is amongst the lowest in the world

9

Corruption

As has been mentioned in an earlier chapter, Hong Kong has a strong anti-corruption regime, headed by the Independent Commission Against Corruption (ICAC). The corruption situation in Hong Kong is under control and the ICAC continues to enjoy a high degree of public confidence.

Human Rights

Hong Kong has a strong commitment to the protection of human rights, based on being a free and open society. The government operates in the full glare of scrutiny by the United Nations treaty monitoring bodies, with its own legislators and a free and active media.

Property Market

This is one of the most discussed subjects in Hong Kong and many locals now find themselves in a negative equity situation when it comes to residential property values. There is a perverse form of inverted snobbery amongst many who have invested in property, and this relates to how much their property has devalued in recent years, particularly since the Asian financial crisis in 1997/98. In 2002, potential buyers were naturally cautious against overcommitting themselves and have turned to the rental market, with an abundance of property to choose from, and can afford to take their time before making a decision.

Activity in the sales market for offices, shopping space, retail premises and industrial property remained weak, although leasing activity was reported to be showing some signs of life. An increased demand for storage premises, for use as logistic centres, seemed to be the best option within the property market, but location and access are all important when deciding on a suitable property.

Drugs

The illegal supply of dangerous drugs is a felony in Hong Kong and, under the Dangerous Drugs Ordinance, the maximum penalty for trafficking in, or manufacturing, dangerous drugs is life imprisonment, and a fine of HK$5 million.

9

Drug abuse is a long standing problem, and Hong Kong's proximity to the Golden Triangle (a principal source of heroin) makes it virtually impossible to control the huge volume of drugs entering Hong Kong everyday by road, rail, sea and air. According to the relevant authorities, there has been considerable success in stopping illicit drug trafficking, breaking up syndicates and making large seizures. Vigorous efforts are made to prevent and detect the exploitation of the financial system for the laundering of drug proceeds, and international cooperation is a key element of investigative work.

Contacts for more specific information on Hong Kong are:

Trade Partners UK – Hong Kong Unit
Website: [www.tradepartners.gov.uk]

Hong Kong Trade Development Council
Email: [london.office@tdc.org.hk]

Hong Kong Economic & Trade Office
Email: [general@hketolondon.gov.uk]

Invest UK (China Team)
Website: [www.invest.uk.com]

Fishy Business

A significant Feng Shui status symbol in an office, or home, is to have a large aquarium, and the bigger the better, housing a single, but "lucky" freshwater tropical fish.

The type of fish is known as AROWANA and it is of the carnivorous species. It will be fed other small fish, river worms or, more usually, small goldfish as these help it to maintain and accentuate its valuable pink glow.

The tank will not contain any plants, rocks, shipwrecks, castles or treasure chests more commonly seen in European fish tanks. Apart from its small, live food, the large fish is entirely on its own, and the ones I have seen are superb works of nature.

They are also very expensive to purchase and a natural talking point amongst owners and visitors

9

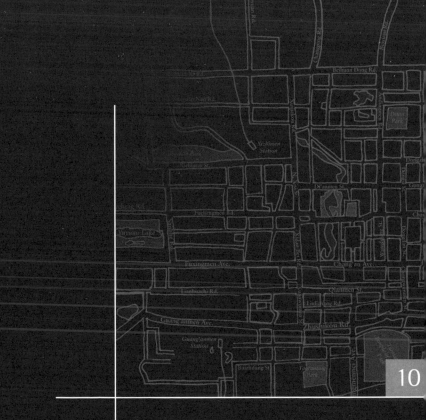

10

a break from business

a break from business

When you have spent most of your waking hours with colleagues and clients, and possibly spent time travelling from one destination to another, the ability to have time to yourself is one of the most precious elements of business travel and an opportunity to recharge your batteries. My business takes me to Hong Kong and China on average six times a year, and I never get tired of visiting either country. For me, Hong Kong is a very special place for a day off and no matter how many times I visit there is always something new to see or experience, and new friends to make.

China

China has some fantastic opportunities for exploring on a day off. The biggest problem is the vastness of the country and the restrictions on travelling outside the established business and tourist areas. The best method of exploration, whilst on a business trip when time is limited, is to embark upon official tours arranged through hotels, or with local friends who can chaperone you and act as tour guides and interpreters at the same time.

10

Beijing

Some of the major tourist attractions in Beijing have been described in Chapter 8, here are some more suggestions: **The Summer Palaces**. Beijing citizens enjoy boating or, in winter, skating on the Fu Hai Lake near the ruins of the **Old Summer Palace**, destroyed during the Second Opium War. There is much to enjoy in the new **Summer Palace**, built by the Empress Dowager Cixi: the beautiful Kunming Lake with its enchanting Seventeen-Arch Bridge, the various Halls, and the **Sea of Wisdom Temple** and the extraordinary Marble Boat.

Outside Beijing

The Ming Tombs make a fascinating excursion and are more accessible from Beijing since the building of the Badeling Expressway. Thirteen Ming Emperors are buried in the valley 50 kilometres northwest of Beijing. You pass the majestic **Avenue of Stone Figures**, 6 kilometres of stone lions, elephants, camels, horses, mythological creatures and imperial dignitaries. Two tombs are open to the public, the **Tomb of the Emperor Yongle**, with the tombs of the concubines buried with him, and the subterranean palace **Tomb of the Emperor**

Wanli, with marble vaulting and golden stones on the floor, and marble thrones for the emperor and his wives. The precious objects found in the tomb, including gold and jade artefacts, blue-and-white Ming porcelain and a fine gold crown, are in separate museums within the complex.

The Western and Eastern Qing Tombs. Also within reach from Beijing. The largest and most beautiful are the Eastern Qing Tombs, set amongst streams, stone bridges and woodland. There are nearly 100 bridges in the complex. **The Tomb of the Emperor Qianlong** is also a subterranean palace, containing vaulted chambers and sculptures and Buddhist inscriptions. **The Tomb of the Empress Dowager Cixi** contains fine stonework and intricate carvings of dragons and phoenixes. The Hall of Eminent Favours contains the Empress's clothes and a robe of sacred verses woven in silk and embroidered in gold thread.

The Imperial Resort at Chengde was built by the Qing emperors to get away from the heat and noise of Beijing. It provides a welcome respite, with pavilions, palaces, Tibetan temples, lakes, trees and gardens among cool mountains and woods 250km from Beijing. It requires two nights' excursion as the train journey from Beijing can take up to 5 hours.

Xi'an

One of the great sights of China and only discovered in 1974 are, of course, the famous **Terracotta Warriors** at Xi'an. You can fly from Beijing to Xi'an, which was the ancient capital of China. The 2000-year-old army of life-size clay warriors, horses and chariots are in a mausoleum outside the city. Built in the 3rd century BC by the Emperor Qin Shi Huangdi, China's despotic first emperor and builder of the Great Wall, 8,000 figures are interred within the outer wall of the emperor's mausoleum, and some of the warriors, each with individual faces, can be viewed from above along constructed walkways.

The vast scale, and the feeling of glimpsing a phantom army from the distant past, makes for an unforgettable experience.

10

Shanghai
See Chapter 9 for suggestions on sight seeing in
Shanghai.

Guangzhou (Canton)
Sights in Guangzhou, not mentioned in Chapter 9.

Guangzhou (Canton), the capital of the Pearl River
Delta, has grown into a vast industrial city with a
population of 10 million (see Chapter 9), but it still has
an old fashioned air. Sights to see are the Chinese
temples, Communist memorials, museums, parks and
Zoo. Guangzhou is known for its famous Cantonese
cuisine and has some of the best restaurants in China.

Shenzhen
Another expanding industrial city, Shenzhen is the first
city you encounter when you cross the border from the
New Territories, but does not yet feature on the tourist
route. Nevertheless, [as I said in Chapter 9], it has
impressive tower blocks, beautiful gardens and parks,
plenty of luxury hotels and masses of restaurants
catering for all tastes and budgets. A huge new
convention and exhibition centre will open in 2003. The
nightlife is sophisticated and golf courses are cheaper
than in Hong Kong. It also has miles of golden sands and
is rapidly becoming one of Southern China's top holiday
resorts.

10

The Three Gorges. More time off is required to do the
Yangtze River Cruise from Chongqing, taking in the
famous and dramatic Three Gorges. The fast flowing
river narrows between high cliffs at Qutang Gorge, and
above Wu Gorge can be seen the 12 high peaks of
Wushan. Xiling Gorge is the longest and most
treacherous of the Three Gorges. The Three Gorges will
virtually vanish when the huge reservoir being
constructed behind the Three Gorges Dam, the Shanxia
Dam at Sandouping, is completed.

Hong Kong
Hong Kong continues to be one of the world's most
important business, tourist and shopping centres in Asia.
A vibrant, cosmopolitan city consisting of a multitude of
spectacularly designed high rise office and apartment
buildings, a large number of well stocked shops,

restaurants and busy streets, Hong Kong is open for business almost 24 hours a day, 7 days a week, throughout the year and it hardly takes time to sleep.

Hong Kong Walk About
The website for numerous tours and attractions in Hong Kong is worth checking out in advance: [www.splendidtours.com]

However, if you enjoy walking it is the best way to experience the sights and sounds of Hong Kong, and the vibrancy of a very active and thriving community. The Hong Kong Tourism Board produces a good free tourists' brochure on Hong Kong, *Museums and Heritage*, which also gives details of Hong Kong's excellent public transport system to help you explore by yourself, which will save you a fortune in expensive guided tours. It is available from the Information Centre (Star Ferry Terminal, Tsim Sha Tsui, Kowloon). I include brief notes on a suggested walking tour to include the main landmarks.

10

If you are staying in Kowloon, take the **Star Ferry** from **Tsim Sha Tsui** to **Central** on Hong Kong Island. The journey across the harbour takes 10 minutes, dodging between tankers, barges, pilot launches, junks, coasters, and other ferries.

Hong Kong Island
Statue Square, the **Legislative Council Chambers (Legco)**, the **Hong Kong Bank**, the **Bank of China**, the **Bank of China Tower**, the **Cenotaph**, the **HSBC building** and the very select **Hong Kong Club**. It is worth window-shopping in **Central** which contains stores of the most famous fashion names in the world. In side alleys off **Queen Street Central** (home of Lane Crawford, Hong Kong's oldest department store) are stalls selling virtually anything and everything imaginable. The **China Products Store** is truly worth a visit, with its many floors of Chinese products and its extraordinary food hall.

Climb up to the world's longest escalator, the **Central - Mid Levels Escalator**, 800 metres long, which winds its way through the buildings. It is said that in Hong Kong you can walk further, off the ground, than anywhere else in the world.

Wanchai, (or Wan Chai) with Hong Kong's oldest shops, selling everything from songbirds, paintings and teahouses, to the proverbial and genuine kitchen sink, and the "Red Light" district.

The Southorn Playground, Wanchai, where men and women do Tai' chi exercises in the morning, young people play football or basketball and old men play Chinese poker or chess.

At the **Central Plaza** take the lift to the 46th floor to experience a bird's eye view of Victoria Harbour and surrounding districts.

Here are the **Convention and Exhibition Centre** and **Grand Hyatt Hotel** and the **Chinese Arts and Crafts Store**. The nearby **Renaissance Harbour View Hotel** has an excellent open lounge for refreshments while enjoying the harbour view. Finish your tour by taking the Wanchai Star Ferry back to Tsim Sha Tsui.

Tsim Sha Tsui, Kowloon
The familiar **Clock Tower**, a relic of the old railway station, the **Hong Kong Cultural Centre**, the **Hong Kong Space Museum**, and the **Museum of Art**.

Wander along the **Waterfront Promenade** behind the Hong Kong Cultural Centre and enjoy the views across the harbour. Twilight is an especially magical time to see the sun setting in the East and the lights emerging from the famous skyline of the island, and have your photo taken against this famous backdrop.

Ballroom Dancing

The Chinese love to dance, and by dancing, I mean ballroom dancing, especially early in the morning, around breakfast time.

If you are out at the time, don't be surprised to hear western dance band music and some melodic Chinese orchestral music wafting through the streets, especially in the vicinity of the major hotels; and don't be equally surprised to find groups of more senior Chinese couples dancing, generally quite expertly to this music. This is the Chinese version of the 'Tea Dance', but at breakfast time, and I find it quite delightful to watch.

10

Main Attractions of Hong Kong

The Peak, Hong Kong Island. On a clear day, a visit to Victoria Peak, at 552m above sea level, is essential. The Peak Tram runs from Garden Road, Central, steeply up to the Peak daily from 7am until midnight. The views from the Peak Tower (396m) and from the Peak Galleria shopping plaza are stunning. The view is equally spectacular by night, and if you stand on the waterfront promenade near the Clock Tower, Kowloon side, looking up towards the Peak, you will see a constant barrage of flashes from cameras. From both directions, at the Peak or at the waterfront, by day or night, the views across the harbour are breathtaking.

Stanley Market, Hong Kong Island. One of the many colourful street markets and a regular haunt of tourists.

Stanley Fort and the **Military Cemetery** are reminders of wartime suffering and especially the 1941-1945 occupation of Hong Kong by the Japanese Army. Stanley was used as an internment camp during those war years, and more latterly as the British Forces base up until the hand over in 1997.

Wanchai. This is the 'red light' district of Hong Kong Island with a multitude of bars, clubs and restaurants, worth seeing both by day and by night.

Lan Kwai Fong, Central, Hong Kong Island. A trendy area bustling with tourists and locals, with a good collection of restaurants, bars and live music.

'The Noon Day Gun.' The three-pounder is still fired every day at noon precisely in the small garden opposite the Excelsior Hotel, Causeway Bay, Hong Kong Island. The employees of Jardine Matheson & Co, one of the oldest trading houses in Hong Kong, carry on a tradition thought to have first begun to welcome the co-founder, William Jardine. It is immortalised by Noel Coward in his song Mad Dogs and Englishmen: 'In Hong Kong, they strike a Gong, and fire off a Noon Day Gun...'

Another truly English tradition is to take tea in the afternoon at the famous **Peninsular Hotel**, Tsim Sha Tsui, Kowloon, or 'The Pen', whilst being serenaded by a string quartet. The Pen was the scene of the official surrender of Hong Kong by the British to the Japanese in 1941, when the hotel was requisitioned as quarters for Japanese officers.

Ocean Park, Hong Kong Island. This is one of the largest theme parks in South East Asia, featuring aquariums, dolphin shows, rides and giant Pandas from China.

Horseracing at the famous **Happy Valley racecourse**, Hong Kong Island.

Jade Market. Located in Yau Ma Tei, Kowloon, there are about 450 stalls selling jade of all types and quality, shapes and sizes. It is open daily from 10am to 3.30pm, but check opening hours during Chinese New Year holidays. Hong Kong is the world's top jade trading centre.

Bird Garden and **Flower Market**, Mongkok, Kowloon, situated on Yuen Po Street and Flower Market Road is worth a visit, as is the Goldfish Market on Tung Choi Street close by.

Temple Street Night Market, Yau Ma Tei, Kowloon. Teeming with shoppers and hawkers and at its busiest and most colourful from 9 pm to 11 pm. Don't miss the local fortune tellers, opera singers and musicians at the top end.

Kowloon Park. This is an oasis of peace with attractive gardens and also a haven for the most extraordinary collection of wild birds, flying loose, within a city environment.

Tsing Ma Bridge. Travelling to and from Hong Kong International Airport, you will cross the world's longest road and rail suspension bridge.

The Star Ferry. A must for any visit to Hong Kong. It provides the best possible introduction to the city whilst offering magnificent views of the harbour and the towering skyline of the island.

10

10

Star Ferry

The Star Ferry has plied its trade between Kowloon and Hong Kong Island since 1898.

The distinctive green and white ferries, bobbing along on their journeys, dodging between heavy water borne traffic of barges with cranes, coastal cargo boats, large passenger ferries, cruise liners, and other faster ferry craft heading for the islands, are a delight to travel on. It must be one of the best and most spectacular ferry rides in the world as it gives passengers a chance to experience the vista of Hong Kong from a distance.

When travelling from Tsim Sha Tsui on Kowloon side across to either Central or Wanchai on the Island, you are confronted with the view of some of the world's most famous tower blocks rising from the water front between Central and Causeway Bay, with the hills and The Peak as a backdrop. On a clear evening, from dusk, as you make this journey, you will see the constant flash of cameras from The Peak, recording the view of the tower blocks from above and the harbour and mainland in the distance. From the ferry, you will see the fantastic kaleidoscopic colours of the illuminations of the buildings, and, in many cases, these colours frequently change and the effects are stunning.

A single journey costs just over HK$ 2.00 If you travel on the top deck and it must be one of the best value-for-money sightseeing tours, ever. It is slightly cheaper to travel on the lower deck, and this is also an experience.

The Star Ferries are just one of 10 ferry operators in Hong Kong and in 2000, the total passengers carried by these operators amounted to 56,139,000.

Peking Road. Tourist guides tend to promote Lan Fai Kwong in Central as the trendy area, but I think the Peking Road and surrounding streets in Tsim Sha Tsui, Kowloon, have just as much to offer. There are shops selling fruit, gifts, electronics, fashion goods, watches, handbags, medicines, also bureaux de change, bars and restaurants — in fact, all life is there on the street. The four floors of HMV are packed with the latest CDs, VCDs and DVDs, all of genuine origin and good prices, and there are plenty of gifts in the **Yue Hwa Chinese Products store**. And you can take a breather in the DeliFrance Coffee Shop in the **Hyatt Regency Hotel**.

Massage
A favourite pastime of Hong Kong business people after a busy day is a massage. In Hong Kong there are good, genuine and safe Health Clubs and Spas (not to be confused with Far Eastern seedy massage parlours), where you can relax with tea, have a manicure, pedicure, sauna, steam or plunge bath, and have an excellent massage lasting nearly one hour. Reflexology and Chinese Foot Massage is also available: go for the soft version as that will be less painful on the feet.

'The Land Between'
There is more to Hong Kong than just the city and business districts on the island and the mainland. **The New Territories,** between the Kowloon Hills and the boundary with Mainland China, is an enormously diverse suburban area full of contrasts, a blend of tradition and modern. More than a century ago the area was entirely rural with small villages, paddy fields and banana plantations. It was home to the Hakka people who farmed rice and tea and to the fishermen who worked from the many small coastal villages scattered around the extensive coastline of the New Territories.

The Hong Kong Tourism Board operate full and half day tours to 'The Land Between' tel +852 2368 7112, or fax +852 2721 9021.
Website: [www.DiscoverHongKong.com]

Island Trips
If you have the time, it is well worth visiting the different islands of Cheung Chau, Lantau and Lamma. The ferry ride itself is interesting, passing through busy shipping lanes, with a multitude of cargo vessels, tankers, barges with cranes and sometimes naval vessels.

Lantau Island. Here you can visit Silvermine Bay and also the Giant Buddha at Po Lin Monastery, the world's largest seated, outdoor bronze Buddha.

10

Lamma Island. The village of Yung Shue Wan on Lamma is a mass of waterfront restaurants specialising in seafood of all shapes, sizes and species, and narrow streets full of stores, local craft shops, bars and more restaurants. On the way to the beach you can see banana plantations, lush vegetation and butterflies of all colours and sizes. Take a steep climb up to the **Han Lok Yuen Restaurant** (Tel: +852 2982 0608; Fax: +852 2982 2564) where tables on the terrace overlook the sea - it is one of the best and most relaxing places to eat in the whole of Hong Kong.

Fishy Tale

On most occasions when you dine out in Hong Kong, fish will be on the menu, and this will usually be the whole fish, either steamed or grilled. There is a well-established superstition within the fishing community, that whilst eating the fish, it should never be turned over as this will cause a fishing boat to capsize. The bones should be removed after the top half has been consumed, to expose the rest of the flesh.

10

A Favourite Hotel

The Royal Garden Hotel, Tsim Sha Tsui East, Kowloon, has excellent facilities, is well located, and relatively quiet — which can be a blessing in Hong Kong. It boasts the best Japanese restaurant in town, the **Inagiku,** with Tempura Bar, Shushi dishes and Teppanyaki food in a splendid Zen setting. It also boasts the best Italian restaurant in town, **Sabatini,** which serves fine French and Italian wines, and the **Royal Garden Chinese Restaurant,** which offers various styles of Chinese cooking, from the spicy Sichuan to the nouvelle cuisine of Hong Kong and Canton — although you will need a generous business account to eat in either establishment. It also has the popular **Martini Bar** and the **Falcon Bar,** which has a live band and is one of the 'in places' for the locals. The hotel has a Business Centre, an excellent rooftop swimming pool, covered by a 'bubble' in winter months, an outdoor tennis court and well equipped gymnasium.

(For a list of hotels in Hong Kong, see Chapter 9 or Appendix 1.)

Some Dim Sum

Dim Sum is one of the staple diets of daytime diners in Hong Kong, and in most Dim Sum restaurants the selection of dishes is paraded in front of you on trolleys. Dim Sum is usually served from early morning to late afternoon, with a good Chinese tea.

The literal translation of Dim Sum is 'small heart' or 'to touch the heart' and whilst there are probab;y more than 2,000 different dishes, restaurants in Hong Kong usually offer between 100-150, as they concentrate on selling the more popular, fast moving items.

Dim Sum is served in steaming, sodden, bamboo baskets and as you choose a dish, a card on your table will be stamped at the apprporiate place, and you are charged per dish when you settle the bill.

Some restaurants have Dim Sum menus, but the more traditional places have 'trolley dollies' dispensing dishes, and I have felt sometimes, they are on commission for what they sell, as they can appear quite dogmatic in what you should choose to eat.

Some of the restaurants that specialise in Dim Sum are brightly decorated in red and gold, as these are considered lucky colours, and also the ambience can be noisy and lively. It all adds to the flavour and experience of eating in Hong Kong.

10

Bars and Restaurants in Hong Kong

Hong Kong is unique in offering cheap good local food courts where a dish of noodles or soup will cost no more than HK$30, or you can dine at some of the world's best and most expensive restaurants, some of which have already been mentioned.

A well hidden gem is **Wu Kong Shanghai Restaurant** in a basement in Peking Road, Tsim Sha Tsui, very popular, serving good quality food at reasonable prices in a pleasant environment. Tel: +852 2366 7244. Website: [www.wukong.com.hk] Along the road is the Irish bar, **Delaney's,** which has televised sporting events, good draught beer and decent sized portions of traditional pub fare.

Visit the sumptuous **Jumbo Floating Restaurant** in Aberdeen Harbour, Hong Kong Island, with its decor of Chinese emperor's throne rooms, very popular with tourists. Have your photograph taken dressed as a Chinese Emperor – that should be one for the company magazine! Website: [www.jumbo.com.hk]

Be entertained while eating at the first class **Peking Garden Restaurant**, Star House, Tsim Sha Tsui, which offers authentic Peking cuisine together with demonstrations of noodle making, carving Peking Duck and the Beggar's Chicken Clay breaking ceremony. Tel: +852 2735 8211; fax: +852 2730 9830.

A traditional restaurant which has been in Hong Kong longer than most people can remember is **Jimmy's Kitchen** in Wyndham Street, Central and Ashley Road, off Peking Road, Tsim Sha Tsui. Worth a visit for good food, decent wine list and unobtrusive service. Tel: or +852 2526 5293 or +852 2376 0327.

To round off the day, go to **Ned Kelly's Last Stand**, Ashley Road, off Peking Road, which serves traditional pub food and has a jazz band from 9.30 pm onwards. A good place to sit and listen to live music in a relaxed and humorous atmosphere, with unexpected 'jam sessions' from members of symphony orchestras or naval bands visiting Hong Kong. Expats of varying nationalities frequent Ned Kelly's. Try to avoid sitting too near the band as it may take several days to regain your hearing.

For an acceptable pint of English beer, try the **Mad Dogs** pub, Lan Kwai Fong, Hong Kong Island, which serves traditional English food and is a favourite amongst the expat community.

Macau

Less frenetic than Hong Kong and retaining the charm of its Portuguese past, Macau is a pleasant island to explore and to enjoy the splendid mixture of baroque Catholic churches, old colonial buildings and fortresses, and ancient Chinese temples. Although its population is 95 per cent Chinese, it is known for its harmonious mix of East and Western culture. Its main attraction for tourists is its nightlife and casinos.

10

A1

Appendix One

A directory of useful telephone numbers and contact details.

Emergencies

	PRC	HK SAR
Ambulance	120	999
Police	110	999
Fire	119	999
Tourist Hotline	*t:* 10 6513 0828	*t:* 2807 6177

Foreigners Section of the Beijing

Public Security Bureau (PSB)   *t:* 10 6525 5486

Telephone Services
Local Telephone Information

	114	1083
Time Check	117	
Weather Information	121	
Post Code Check	*t:* 10 6303 7131	

Embassies & Consulates

	Beijing	HK SAR
Australia	*t:* 10 6532 2331	*t:* 2827 8881
Canada	*t:* 10 6532 3536	*t:* 2810 4321
United Kingdom	*t:* 10 6532 1961	*t:* 2901 3182
USA	*t:* 10 6532 6057	*t:* 2523 9011

	Shanghai
Australia	*t:* 6437 4580
Canada	*t:* 6279 8400
United Kingdom	*t:* 6279 7650
USA	*t:* 6433 6880

	Guangzhou
Australia	*t:* 8331 2738
United Kingdom	*t:* 8333 6623
USA	*t:* 8888 8911

Hospitals
Beijing
Beijing Union Hospital
t: 10 6513 5002

A1

Beijing United Family Hospital
t: 10 6433 3960

International Medical Centre
t: 10 6465 1561

Sino-Japanese Friendship Hospital
  t: 10 6422 1122

Shanghai
General   *t:* 324 0100

Guangzhou
General   *t:* 6333 090

Dental Association   *t:* 2528 5327

HK SAR
Contact the Embassy or Consulate for local information

Chambers of Commerce
Beijing   **HK SAR**

United Kingdom
t: 10 6593 6611   *t:* 2824 2211

E U Chamber of Commerce
t: 10 6462 2067

China Britain Business Council
t: 6593 6611

United Kingdom
t: 020 7826 5176

Shanghai
t: 6218 5183

Shenzhen
t: 5218 7157

Hong Kong Trade Development Council
HK SAR
t: 2584 4333

United Kingdom
t: 020 7616 9500

British Council

                            HK SAR
t: 10 6501 1903   *t:* 2913 5100

A1

Airlines

	PRC	HK SAR
Capital Airport (Beijing) Information		
	t: 10 6456 3604	
Air China	*t:* 10 6601 7755	*t:* 2861 0322
Air France	*t:* 10 6588 1388	*t:* 2524 8145
Air India		*t:* 2521 4321
Alitalia	*t:* 10 6561 0375	*t:* 2523 7047
All Nippon Airways		
	t: 10 6505 3311	*t:* 2810 7100
Asiana Airlines	*t:* 10 6468 1118	*t:* 2769 7782
British Airways	*t:* 10 6512 4070	*t:* 2868 0303
Canadian Airlines International		
	t: 10 6468 2001	*t:* 2868 3123
Cathay Pacific Airways		*t:* 2747 1888
China Airlines		*t:* 2868 2299
China Eastern Airlines		*t:* 2861 0288
China Southern Airlines		*t:* 2865 2576
Delta Airlines		*t:* 2769 8452
Dragonair	*t:* 10 6505 4343	*t:* 2590 1188
Emirates Airline		*t:* 2769 8533
Evergreen Airlines		*t:* 2382 7373
Finnair	*t:* 10 6512 7180	
Garuda Indonesia	*t:* 10 6505 2901	
Japan Airlines	*t:* 10 6513 0888	*t:* 2523 0081
KLM Royal Dutch Airlines		
	t: 10 6505 3505	*t:* 2808 2111
Korean Air	*t:* 10 6505 0088	*t:* 2368 6221
Lufthansa	*t:* 10 6465 4488	*t:* 2868 2313
Malaysia Airlines		
	t: 10 6505 2681	*t:* 2821 8181
Mongolian Airlines		
	t: 10 6507 9297	
Northwest Airlines		
	t: 10 6505 3505	*t:* 2810 4288
Polish Airlines	*t:* 10 6500 7215	
Pakistan International Airlines		
	t: 10 6505 1681	*t:* 2366 4770
Philippine Airlines		*t:* 2369 4521
Qantas Airways	*t:* 10 6467 4794	*t:* 2524 2101
Royal Brunei Airways		*t:* 2747 1888
Royal Nepal Airways		*t:* 2369 9151
SAS Scandinavian Airlines		
	t: 10 6518 3738	*t:* 2865 1370

A1

Singapore Airlines	**t:** 10 6505 2233	**t:** 2520 2233
South African Airways		**t:** 2722 5768
SwissAir	**t:** 10 6512 3555	**t:** 2861 8888
Thai Airways International		
	t: 10 6460 8899	**t:** 2529 5601
United Airlines	**t:** 10 6463 1111	**t:** 2810 4888
VARIG Brazilian Airlines		**t:** 2511 1234
Virgin Atlantic Airways		**t:** 2532 3030

Hotels

Beijing

China World Hotel ★★★★★
located close to all main business areas
t: 10 6505 2266

Crown Plaza Hotel ★★★★★
located in Wangfujing shopping area
t: 662 913 6030

Holiday Inn Lido Hotel ★★★★★
near the International Exhibition Centre
t: 10 6437 6688

Jing Guang New World ★★★★★
located close to the embassy district, business and
shopping areas
t: 10 6597 8888

Shangri-La Hotel ★★★★★
close to the financial district
t: 10 6841 2211

Sheraton Great Wall Hotel ★★★★★
in the diplomatic area and close to commercial centres
t: 10 6590 5566

Beijing Movenpick Airport Hotel ★★★★
the best of the airport hotels
t: 10 6459 0855/6/7

Capital Hotel ★★★★
right in the city centre
t: 10 6512 9988

Jian Guo Hote ★★★★ l
located 4km from the city centre
t: 10 6500 2233

Novotel Peace Hotel ★★★
located on Morrison Hill Road
t: 10 6512 8833

A1

Songhe Hotel ★★★
near the busy Wangfujing shopping area
t: 10 6513 8822

Shanghai

Portman Shangri-La Hotel ★★★★★
centrally located
t: 21 6279 8888

J.C. Mandarin Hotel ★★★★★
located in the shopping and tourist district
t: 21 6279 1888

Jinjiang Tower Hotel ★★★★★
situated in the commercial district
t: 21 6258 2882

Hilton Hotel ★★★★★
city centre location and near major commercial and
shopping areas
t: 21 6248 0000

Peace Hotel ★★★★★
close to the Bund and Huangpu River
t: 21 6322 3855

Sofitel Hyland Hotel ★★★★
located in the famous walking mile with shops,
restaurants, etc.
t: 21 6351 5888

Guangzhou

China Hotel ★★★★★
located in the city centre
t: 20 8666 6888

Dongfang Hotel ★★★★★
located in the city centre and set in large, traditional
gardens
t: 20 8666 9900

White Swan Hotel ★★★★★
situated on Shamian Island, overlooking the Pearl River
t: 20 8188 6968

Garden Hotel ★★★★★l
well located for airport and railway station
t: 20 8333 8989

A1

Landmark Hotel ★★★★
in the city centre overlooking the Pearl River
t: 20 8355 5988

Full details of these hotels, and many others, can be
obtained by visiting the website:
[www.direct-rooms-china.com]

Hong Kong
The two main locations for hotels are Hong Kong Island
and Kowloon.

For the hotels listed, E = economy price, M = medium
price and L = luxury price categories.

Hong Kong Island
Causeway Bay

Metropark Hotel – E
t: 852 2600 1000

Regal Hong Kong Hotel – L
t: 852 2890 6633

Rosedale on the Park – L
t: 852 2127 8888

Central

Island Shangri-La Hong Kong Hotel – L
t: 852 2877 3838

Mandarin Oriental – L
t: 852 2522 0111

JW Marriott Hotel – L
t: 852 2810 8366

The Ritz Carlton Hotel – L
t: 852 2877 6666

Happy Valley

Emperor (Happy Valley) Hotel – M
t: 852 2893 3693

North Point

Ibis North Point Hotel – E
t: 852 2588 1111

Newton Hotel – E
t: 852 2807 2333

A1

City Garden Hotel – E
t: 852 2887 2888

Wanchai

Novotel Century HK Hotel – M
t: 852 2598 8888

Grand Hyatt HK Hotel – L
t: 852 2588 1234

Harbour View International House – E
t: 852 2802 0111

Renaissance Harbour View Hotel – L
t: 852 2802 8888

The Warney Hotel – E
t: 852 2861 1000

The Charterhouse Hotel – E
t: 852 2833 5566

Kowloon
Tsim Sha Tsui and Tsim Sha Tsui East

The Peninsula HK – L
t: 852 2929 2888; ext: 3366

Kowloon Shangri-La Hotel – L
t: 852 2721 0283

The Sheraton HK Hotel – L
t: 852 2369 1111

Hyatt Regency HK Hotel – L
t: 852 2311 1234

The Royal Garden Hotel – L
t: 852 2721 5215

Hotel Inter-Continental HK – L
t: 852 2721 5161

Great Eagle Hotel – L
t: 852 2375 1133

New World Renaissance Hotel – M
t: 852 2369 4111

Holiday Inn Golden Mile Hotel – M
t: 852 2369 3111

A1

Kowloon Hotel – E
t: 852 2929 2888

BP International House (The Boys Scouts) – E
t: 852 2376 1111

Empire Kowloon – E
t: 852 2685 3000

Guangdong Hotel – E
t: 662 913 6030

There are many websites available giving full details, and
much more, of the hotels and deals available:
[www.hongkonghotels.net]

A1

Appendix Two

Appendix two

Chinese Language

It has already been mentioned that in China there is one common written language but a vast number of dialects.

The national language is Mandarin (Putonghua) which is based on the Beijing dialect, whereas in the south of China and Hong Kong, Cantonese is widely spoken. A person from Hong Kong or Guangzhou would have difficulty communicating orally with someone from Beijing although they could write to each other.

There is, however, a form of standard Chinese, based on the pronunciation of the northern dialects, and in particular, the Beijing dialect. This is referrred to as Pinyin and is basically the phonetic transcription of the language of the Han people.

It is perhaps reassuring to the visitor to learn that English is increasingly being used in China, but it is useful to know a few familiar phrases, your Chinese colleagues will be flattered and impressed, and you will know if they are talking about you.

Putonghua has four tones, spoken with emphasis. The first tone is high and level, the second starting low and rising, the third falling and then rising, and the fourth falling. However, there are some variations in the tones, and it really depends on the dialect, intonation and education of the natural speaker.

A2

Useful Phrases

Pinyin Alphabet

a (a)   Vowel as in *far*
b (p)   Consonant as in *be*
c (ts')   Consonant as in *chip*; strongly aspirated
d (t)   Consonant as in *do*
e (e)   Vowel as in *her*
f (f)   Consonant as in *foot*
g (k')   Consonant as in *go*
h (h)   Consonant as in *her*; strongly aspirated
i (i)   Vowel as in *eat* or as in *sir* (when in syllables beginning with c, ch, r, s, sh, z and zh.)
j (ch)   Consonant as in *jeep*
k (k')   Consonant as in *kind*, strongly aspirated
l (l)   Consonant as in *land*
m (m)   Consonant as in *me*
n (n)   Consonant as in *now*

o (o)   Vowel as in *law*
p (p')   Consonant as in *par*; strongly aspirated
q (ch')   Consonant as in *cheek*
r (j)   Consonant as in *right*; (not rolled) or pronounced as *z* in *azure*
s (s, ss, sz)   Consonant as in *sister*
sh (sh) Consonant as in *shore*
t (t')   Consonant as in *top*; strongly aspirated
u (u)   Vowel as in *too*; also as in French *tu* or the German Mūnchen
v (v)   Consonant used only to produce foreign words, national minority words, and local dialects
w (w)   Semi-vowel in syllables beginning with u when not preceded by a consonant, as in *want*
x (hs)   Consonant as in *she*
y   Semi-vowel in syllables beginning with i or u when not preceded by a consonant, as in *yet*
z (ts, tz)   Consonant as in *adze*
zh (ch)   Consonant as in *jump*

I, me; mine	wǒ (*waw*); wǒde (*wah-duh*)
You; your	nǐ (*nee*); nǐde (*nee-duh*)
He, it/she	tā (*tah*) / tā (*tah*)
His, its/hers	tāde (*tah-duh*) / tāde (*tah-duh*)
We, us	wǒmen (*waw-mun*)
You (pl.)	nǐmen (*nee-mun*)
They, them (m./f.)	tāmen (*tah-mun*) / tāmen (*tah-mun*)
Their (m./f.)	tāmende (*tah-mun-duh*) / tāmende (*tah-mun-duh*)
Hello, how are you?	nǐ hǎo; (*nee hao*); nǐ hǎo ma (*nee hao mah*
Good morning	zǎo (*dzao*); zǎo ān (*dzao an*)
Good evening	wǎn ān (*wahn an*)
Good-bye	zaì jiàn (*dzai jee-en*)
I don't understand	wǒ bù dǒng (*waw boo doong*)
Yes, I agree; correct	shì (*shir*); dùi (*doo-ay*)
I don't agree	bù tóngyì (*boo toong-yee*)
Please	qǐng (*ching*)
Thank you; many thanks	xiè xie (*shee-eh shee-eh*); dūo xiè (*dwaw shee-eh*)
It's nothing (don't mention it)	bú kèqì (*boo kuh-chee*)
I'm sorry	duì bùqǐ (*doo-ay boo chee*)

OK, you can	kěyǐ (*kuh-ee*)
Not OK, you can't	bú kěyǐ (*boo kuh-ee*)
Not bad, so-so	hái kěyǐ (*hi kuh-ee*)
Good; very good	hǎo (*hao*); hěn hǎo (*hun hao*)
No (not) good	bù hǎo (*boo hao*)
Thank you but I...	xiè xie, wǒ... (*she-eh, waw...*)

	am unable to	bù néng (*boo nung*)
	don't want to	bú yào (*boo yao*)
	don't like	· bù xǐhuān (*boo shee-hwahn*

Pleased; happy	huānxǐ (*hwahn-shee*)
Very; extremely	hěn (*hun*); fēicháng (*fay-chahng*)
Slow	màn (*man*)
Fast	kuài (*kwhy*)
Hot	rè (*ruh*)
Cold	lěng (*lung*)
Who?	shúi (*shway*)
When is...?	shénma shíhòu (*shum-mah shir-hoe*)
Where...;...is where...?	shénma dìfang... (*shum-mah dee fahng...*); ...zài nǎlǐ (*...dzai nah-lee*)
Friend péngyǒu	(*pung-yo*)
Friendly	yǒu hǎo (*yo-hao*)
May I please ask your name?	
	qǐngwèn guìxìng (*ching-win gway-shing*)
My name is...	wǒ jiaò (*waw djeeow*)
I am	wio shì (*waw shir*)

	American	měiguórén (*may-gwaw run*)
	Australian	àudàlìyǎrén (*ow-dah-lee-ah run*)
	British	yīnggúorén (*ying-gwaw run*)
	Canadian	jiānadaren (*jee-ah-nah-dah run*)

Travel

Right	yòu (*yo*)
Left	zǔo (*dzwaw*)
Front	qián (*chee-en*)
Back	hòu (*hoe*)
Luggage	xínglǐ (*shing-lee*)
Customs	hǎiguān (*hye-gwan*)
Car	qìchē (*chee-chuh*)
Bus	gōnggòng qìchē (*gung-gung cheecheh*)
Taxi	chūzū qìchē (*choo-dzoo chee-cheh*)

A2

Airport	fēijīchǎng (*fay-jee-chahng*)
Railway station	huǒchēzhàn (*hwaw-cheh jan*)
Bicycle	zìxíngchē (*dze-sing-cheh*)
Bicycle rental	chūzū zìxíngchē (*choo-dzoo-dze-sing-cheh*)

At the Hotel

Hotel	lǔguǎn (*lu-gwan*)
Room	fángjiān (*fahng-jee-en*)
Key	yàoshi (*yao shir*)
Floor	lóu (*lo*)
Lift (elevator)	diàntī (*dee-en tee*)
Stairs	lóutī (*low-tee*)
Telephone	diànhuà (*dee-en-hwa*)
Light (electric)	diàndēng (*dee-endung*)
Fridge	bīng xiāng (*bing-shee-ahng*)
Television	diàn shì (*dee-en-shr*)
Radio	shōuyīnjī (*show-yin-gee*)
Air-conditioning	kōngtiáo/lěngqì (*kawng-tyaw/lung-chee*)
Laundry	xǐyīdian (*shee yee dee-en*)
Toilet	cèsuǒ (*tse-swo*)
Men's	nán (*nahn*)
Women's	nǔ (*new*)
Bath	xǐzǎo (*shee-dzao*)
Water	shǔi (*shway*)
Please come in	qǐng jinlai (*ching jeen-lye*)
(Please) wait a moment	
	děngyīdeng (*dung-yee-dung*)
Sleep	shùizháo (*shway-jao*)
Bed	chuáng (*chew-ahng*)
Sheets	chuáng dān (*chew-ahng don*)
Towel	maó jīn (*mao jeen*)
Clean	gān jìng (*gahn jeeng*)
Not clean	bù gān jìng (*boo gahn jeeng*)
Have	yǒu (*yo*)
Not have	méi yǒu (*may yo*)
Hotel restaurant	cān tīng (*kahn teeng*)
Hotel shop	xiǎomàibù (*shao my boo*)
Post office	yóujú (*yo-joo*)
barber shop	lǐfǎdìan (*lee-fah-dee-en*)

A2

Sightseeing

Welcome	huānyǐng (*hwahn-ying*)
We would like to visit a...	
	wǒmen yào qù... (*waw-mun yao chu*)
See, watch	kàn (*kahn*)
Factory	gōngchǎng (*goong chahng*)
Museum	bówùguǎn (*baw-woo-gwan*)
Park	gōngyuán (*goong-yoo-ahn*)
School	xuéxiào (*shoo-eh shee-ow*)
Shop	shāngdiàn (*shahng-dee-en*)
University	dàxué (*da shoo-eh*)
Temple	sìmiào (*suh-myao*)
Buddhist temple	sì (*see*)
Confucian temple	miào (*mee-yao*)
Daoist temple	guàn (*gwahn*)
Take a picture	zhàoxiàng (*jao shee-ahng*)

Shopping

Antique	gǔdǒng (*goo-doong*)
Artworks	yìshùpǐn (*ee-shoo-peen*)
Book	shū (*shoo*)
Bookshop	shūdiàn (*shoo dee-en*)
Department store	bǎihuòshāngdiàn (*bye-hwaw shahng-dee-en*)
Handicrafts; art	gōngyìpǐn (*goong yee-peen*)
Stamps	yóupiaò (*yo-pee-ow*)
How much (money)?	
	duōshǎo qián (*dwaw-shao chee-en*)
Expensive	guì (*gway*)
Cheap	piányi (*pee-en yee*)
Change	língqián (leeng-chh-en*)
Where can I buy...?	
	zài nǎlǐ kěyǐ mǎi (*dzai nah-lee kuh-yee my*)
I would like that...	wǒ yào nèige... (*waw-yao nay-guh...*)
black one	hēide (*hay-duh*)
blue one	lánde (*lahn-duh*)
green one	lùde (*lee-yu-duh*)
red one	hóngde (*hoong-duh*)
white one	báide (*bye-duh*)
yellow one	huǎngde (*hoo-ahng-duh*)
brown one	zōngde (*dzong-de*)
grey one	hūide (*hoo-ay-duh*)

A2

Food

I am hungry	wǒ èle (*waw uh-luh*)
I am thirsty	wǒ kěle (*waw kuh-luh*)
Eat	chī (*chir*)
Drink	hē (*huh*)
Restaurant	fànguǎn (*fahn gwan*)
Breakfast	zǎocān (*dzao-tsahn*)
	zǎofàn (*dzao-fan*)
Lunch	wǔcān (*woo-tsahn*)
	wǔfàn (*woo-fan*)
Dinner	wǎncān (*wahn-tsahn*)
	wǎnfàn (*wahn-fan*)
Snack/dessert	diǎnxīn (*dee-en sheen*)
Chopsticks	kuàizi (*kwhy-dzih*)
Knife	dāo (*dao*)
Fork	chā (*chah*)
Spoon	tāngchi (*tahng-chir*)

What is your speciality?

yǒu shénma tèbiéde hǎochi
(*yo shummahtuh-bee-eh-duh hao-chir*)

I've had enough to eat

chībǎole (*chir-bao-luh*)

The food was delicious

hěn hǎochī (*hun hao-chir*)

Cheers!	gānbēi (*gahn-bei*)
Water (cold)	liángkāishǔi (*lee-ahng kai-shway*)
Coffee	kāfēi (*kah-fay*)
Tea	chà (*chah*)
Beer	píjiǔ (*pee-jee-oh*)
Beef	niúròu (*nee-oh row*)
Chicken	jī (*jee*)
Duck	yāzi (*yah-dzih*)
Pork	zhūroù (*jew-ro*)
Fish	yú (*yu*)
Shrimp	xiā (*shee-yah*)
Eggs	jīdàn (*jee-dan*)
Rice	fàn (*fahn*)
Vegetables	qīngcài (*ching-tsye*)
Soup	tāng (*tahng*)
Fruit	shǔiguǒ (*shway-gwaw*)

Apple	píngguǒ (*ping-gwaw*)
Banana	xiāngjiāo (*shee-ahng-je-ow*)
Orange	júzi (*ju-dzih*)
Peach	táozi (*tao-dzih*)
Pear	lízi (*lee-dzih*)
Watermelon	xīguā (*shee-gwa*)

Ice-cream   bīngqílín (*bing-chee-leen*)
Western food   xīcān (*shee-tsahn*)
Vegetarian   chīsù (*chir soo*)
Sweet   tián (*tee-en*)
Sour   suān (*swan*)
Bitter   kǔ (*koo*)
Spicy (hot)   là (*lah*)

Health care/Medicine
Medicine   yào (*yao*)
Pharmacy   yàodiàn (*yao deen-en*)
Where can I find medicine?
                     nǎlǐ yǒu yào mǎi (*nah-lee yo yao my*)
Aspirin   āsīpǐlín (*ah-suh-pee-leen*)
I have a cold   wǒ gǒnmàole (*waw gone-mao-luh*)
I don't feel well   wǒ bù shūfu (*waw boo shoo-foo*)
I am ill   wǒ bìngle (*waw beeng-luh*)
Call a doctor   qǐng yīshēng lái (*ching yee-shung lye*)
Dentist   yáyī (*yah-yee*)
Hospital   yīyuàn (*yee yoo-en*)
Headache   tóutòng (*toe-tuhng*)
Toothache   yátòng (*yah-tuhng*)
Dizziness   tóuyùn (*toe yew-win*)
Diarrhoea   lādùzi (*lah doo-dzi*)
Stomach sickness   wèibìng (*way-bing*)
Stomach pain   wèitòng (*way-tuhng*)
It hurts me here   wǒ zhèli tòng (*waw juh-lee tuhng*)

Time

What time is it?   jǐdǐan zhong (*jee dee-en joong*)

[number] o'clock   ...dian zhōng (*...dee-en joong*)
Morning   zǎoshàng (*dzao-shahng*)
Midday   zhōngwǔ (*joong-woo*)
Evening   wǎnshàng (*wahn-shahng*)
Yesterday   zuótiān (*dzwaw-tee-en*)
Today   jīntiān (*jeen-tee-en*)
Tomorrow   míngtiān (*ming-tee-en*)
Day   tiān (*tee-en*)
Month   yuè (*yweh*)
Year   nián (*nee-en*)

A2

Numbers

One	yī (*yee*)
Two	èr (*are*)
Three	sān (*san*)
Four	sì (*suh*)
Five	wǔ (*woo*)
Six	liù (*lee-oh*)
Seven	qī (*chee*)
Eight	bā (*bah*)
Nine	jiǔ (*jee-oh*)
Ten	shí (*shir*)
Eleven	shíyī (*shir-yee*)
Twelve	shíèr (*shir-yee*)
Thirteen	shísān (*shir-san*)
Fourteen	shísì (*shir-suh*)
Twenty	èrshí (*are-shir*)
Thirty	sānshí (*san-shir*)
One hundred	yībǎi (*yee-bye*)
One thousand	yīqiān (*yee-chee-en*)

A2

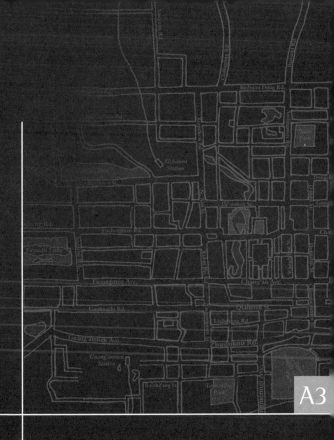

A3

commercial support
for US companies

Appendix three

Directory of Export Assistance Centers

Cities in capital letters are centres which combine the export promotion and trade finance service of the Department of Commerce, the Export-Import Bank, the Small Business Administration and the Agency of International Development.

ALABAMA

Birmingham, Alabama - George Norton, Director
950 22nd Street North, Room 707, ZIP 35203
t: (205) 731-1331   *f:* (205) 731-0076

ALASKA

Anchorage, Alaska - Charles Becker, Director
550 West 7th Ave., Suite 1770, ZIP: 99501
t: (907) 271-6237   *f:* (907) 271-6242

ARIZONA

Phoenix, Arizona - Frank Woods, Director
2901 N. Central Ave., Suite 970, ZIP 85012
t: (602) 640-2513   *f:* (602) 640-2518

CALIFORNIA - LONG BEACH

Joseph F Sachs, Director
Mary Delmege, CS Director
One World Trade Center, Ste. 1670, ZIP: 90831
t: (562) 980-4550   *f:* (562) 980-4561

CALIFORNIA - SAN JOSE

101 Park Center Plaza, Ste. 1001, ZIP: 95113
t: (408) 271-7300   *f:* (408) 271-7307

COLORADO - DENVER

Nancy Charles-Parker, Director
1625 Broadway, Suite 680, ZIP: 80202
t: (303) 844-6623   *f:* (303) 844-5651

CONNECTICUT

Middletown, Connecticut - Carl Jacobsen, Director
213 Court Street, Suite 903 ZIP: 06457-3346
t: (860) 638-6950   *f:* (860) 638-6970

A3

DELAWARE
Served by the Philadelphia, Pennsylvania U.S. Export Assistance Center

FLORIDA - MIAMI
John McCartney, Director
P.O. Box 590570, ZIP: 33159
5600 Northwest 36th St., Ste. 617, ZIP: 33166
t: (305) 526-7425   *f:* (305) 526-7434

GEORGIA - ATLANTA
Samuel Troy, Director
285 Peachtree Center Avenue, NE, Suite 200
ZIP: 30303-1229
t: (404) 657-1900   *f:* (404) 657-1970

HAWAII
Honolulu, Hawaii - Greg Wong, Manager
1001 Bishop St.; Pacific Tower; Suite 1140
ZIP: 96813
t: (808) 522-8040   *f:* (808) 522-8045

IDAHO
Boise, Idaho - James Hellwig, Manager
700 West State Street, 2nd Floor, ZIP: 83720
t: (208) 334-3857   *f:* (208) 334-2783

ILLINOIS - CHICAGO
Mary Joyce, Director
55 West Monroe Street, Suite 2440, ZIP: 60603
t: (312) 353-8045   *f:* (312) 353-8120

INDIANA
Indianapolis, Indiana - Dan Swart, Manager
11405 N. Pennsylvania Street, Suite 106
Carmel, IN, ZIP: 46032
t: (317) 582-2300   *f:* (317) 582-2301

IOWA
Des Moines, Iowa - Allen Patch, Director
601 Locust Street, Suite 100, ZIP: 50309-3739
t: (515) 288-8614   *f:* (515) 288-1437

A3

KANSAS
Wichita, Kansas - George D. Lavid, Manager
209 East William, Suite 300, ZIP: 67202-4001
t: (316) 269-6160   **f:** (316) 269-6111

KENTUCKY
Louisville, Kentucky - John Autin, Director
601 W. Broadway, Room 634B , ZIP: 40202
t: (502) 582-5066   **f:** (502) 582-6573

LOUISIANA
Patricia Holt, Acting Director
365 Canal Street, Suite 1170
New Orleans ZIP: 70130
t: (504) 589-6546   **f:** (504) 589-2337

MAINE
Portland, Maine - Jeffrey Porter, Manager
c/o Maine International Trade Center
511 Congress Street, ZIP: 04101
t: (207) 541-7400   **f:** (207) 541-7420

MARYLAND - BALTIMORE
Michael Keaveny, Director
World Trade Center, Suite 2432
401 East Pratt Street, ZIP: 21202
t: (410) 962-4539   **f:** (410) 962-4529

MASSACHUSETTS - BOSTON
Frank J. O'Connor, Director
164 Northern Avenue
World Trade Center, Suite 307, ZIP: 02210
t: (617) 424-5990   **f:** (617) 424-5992

MICHIGAN - DETROIT
Neil Hesse, Director
211 W. Fort Street, Suite 2220, ZIP: 48226
t: (313) 226-3650   **f:** (313) 226-3657

MINNESOTA - MINNEAPOLIS
Ronald E. Kramer, Director
45 South 7th St., Suite 2240, ZIP: 55402
t: (612) 348-1638   **f:** (612) 348-1650

A3

MISSISSIPPI
Mississippi - Harrison Ford, Manager
704 East Main St., Raymond, MS, ZIP: 39154
t: (601) 857-0128   *f:* (601) 857-0026

MISSOURI - ST LOUIS
Randall J. LaBounty, Director
8182 Maryland Avenue, Suite 303, ZIP: 63105
t: (314) 425-3302   *f:* (314) 425-3381

MONTANA
Missoula, Montana - Mark Peters, Manager
c/o Montana World Trade Center
Gallagher Business Bldg., Suite 257, ZIP: 59812
t: (406) 243-2098   *f:* (406) 243-5259

NEBRASKA
Omaha, Nebraska - Meredith Bond, Manager
11135 "O" Street, ZIP: 68137
t: (402) 221-3664   *f:* (402) 221-3668

NEVADA
Reno, Nevada - Jere Dabbs, Manager
1755 East Plumb Lane, Suite 152, ZIP: 89502
t: (702) 784-5203   *f:* (702) 784-5343

NEW HAMPSHIRE
Portsmouth, New Hampshire - Susan Berry, Manager
17 New Hampshire Avenue, ZIP: 03801-2838
t: (603) 334-6074   *f:* (603) 334-6110

NEW JERSEY
Trenton, New Jersey - Rod Stuart, Director
3131 Princeton Pike, Bldg. #4, Suite 105, ZIP: 08648
t: (609) 989-2100   *f:* (609) 989-2395

NEW MEXICO
New Mexico - Sandra Necessary, Manager
c/o New Mexico Dept. of Economic Development
P.O. Box 20003, Santa Fe, ZIP: 87504-5003
FEDEX:1100 St. Francis Drive, ZIP: 87503
t: (505) 827-0350   *f:* (505) 827-0263

A3

NEW YORK
John Lavelle, Acting Director
6 World Trade Center, Rm. 635, ZIP: 10048
t: (212) 466-5222 *f:* (212) 264-1356

NORTH CAROLINA
Roger Fortner, Director
521 East Morehead Street, Suite 435, Charlotte, ZIP:
28202
t: (704) 333-4886 *f:* (704) 332-2681

NORTH DAKOTA
Served by the Minneapolis, Minnesota Export
AssistanceCenter

OHIIO - CLEVELAND
Michael Miller, Director
600 Superior Avenue, East, Suite 700
ZIP: 44114
t: (216) 522-4750 *f:* (216) 522-2235

OKLAHOMA
Oklahoma City, Oklahoma - Ronald L. Wilson, Director
301 Northwest 63rd Street, Suite 330, ZIP: 73116
t: (405) 608-5302 *f:* (405) 608-4211

OREGON - PORTLAND
Scott Goddin, Director
One World Trade Center, Suite 242
121 SW Salmon Street, ZIP: 97204
t: (503) 326-3001 *f:* (503) 326-6351

PENNSYLVANIA - PHILADELPHIA
Rod Stuart, Acting Director
615 Chestnut Street, Ste. 1501, ZIP: 19106
t: (215) 597-6101 *f:* (215) 597-6123

PUERTO RICO
San Juan, Puerto Rico (Hato Rey) - Vacant, Manager
525 F.D. Roosevelt Avenue, Suite 905
ZIP: 00918
t: (787) 766-5555 *f:* (787) 766-5692

A3

RHODE ISLAND
Providence, Rhode Island - Vacant, Manager
One West Exchange Street, ZIP: 02903
t: (401) 528-5104, *f:* (401) 528-5067

SOUTH CAROLINA
Columbia, South Carolina - Ann Watts, Director
1835 Assembly Street, Suite 172, ZIP: 29201
t: (803) 765-5345   *f:* (803) 253-3614

SOUTH DAKOTA
Siouxland, South Dakota - Cinnamon King, Manager
Augustana College, 2001 S. Summit Avenue
Room SS-44, Sioux Falls, ZIP: 57197
t: (605) 330-4264   *f:* (605) 330-4266

TENNESSEE
Memphis, Tennessee - Ree Russell, Manager
Buckman Hall, 650 East Parkway South, Suite 348
ZIP: 38104.
t: (901) 323-1543   *f:* (901) 320-9128

TEXAS - DALLAS
LoRee Silloway, Director
P.O. Box 420069, ZIP: 75342-0069
2050 N. Stemmons Fwy., Suite 170, ZIP: 75207
t: (214) 767-0542   *f:* (214) 767-8240

UTAH
Salt Lake City, Utah - Stanley Rees, Director
324 S. State Street, Suite 221, ZIP: 84111
t: (801) 524-5116   *f:* (801) 524-5886

VERMONT
Montpelier, Vermont - Susan Murray, Manager
National Life Building, Drawer 20, ZIP: 05620-0501
t: (802) 828-4508   *f:* (802) 828-3258

VIRGINIA
Richmond, Virginia - Helen D. Lee Hwang, Manager
400 North 8th Street, Suite 540, ZIP: 23240-0026
P.O. Box 10026
t: (804) 771-2246   *f:* (804) 771-2390

A3